**Fine WoodWorking** | # Tables and Chairs

Editors of *Fine Woodworking*

The Taunton Press

The Taunton Press
Inspiration for hands-on living®

THE TAUNTON PRESS, INC.
63 South Main Street, PO Box 5506
Newtown, CT 06470-5506
e-mail: tp@taunton.com

EDITOR: Christina Glennon
COPY EDITOR: Candace B. Levy
INDEXER: Jim Curtis
JACKET/COVER DESIGN: carol singer | notice design
INTERIOR DESIGN: carol singer | notice design
LAYOUT: Kimberly Shake

Fine Woodworking® is a trademark of The Taunton Press, Inc., registered in the U.S. Patent and Trademark Office.

The following names/manufacturers appearing in *Fine Woodworking Tables and Chairs* are trademarks:
Amana®, Freud®, Masonite®, Microplane®, Minwax®, Tried & True™, Watco®, Waterlox®

LIBRARY OF CONGRESS CATALOGING-IN-PUBLICATION DATA IN PROGRESS

ISBN# 978-1-56158-100-9

PRINTED IN THE UNITED STATES OF AMERICA
10 9 8 7 6 5 4 3 2 1

This book is compiled from articles that originally appeared in *Fine Woodworking* magazine. Unless otherwise noted, costs listed were current at the time the article first appeared.

ABOUT YOUR SAFETY: Working wood is inherently dangerous. Using hand or power tools improperly or ignoring safety practices can lead to permanent injury or even death. Don't try to perform operations you learn about here (or elsewhere) unless you're certain they are safe for you. If something about an operation doesn't feel right, don't do it. Look for another way. We want you to enjoy the craft, so please keep safety foremost in your mind whenever you're in the shop.

ACKNOWLEDGMENTS

Special thanks to the authors, editors, art directors, copy editors, and other staff members of *Fine Woodworking* who contributed to the development of the chapters in this book.

Contents

Introduction

There is no more useful and ubiquitous piece of furniture than the table. Whether in front, behind, or beside a sofa, whether tucked into a hallway or dominating a dining area, the table is where life happens. Therefore, there is no better place to show off your woodworking skills.

Maybe the most useful piece of all is a dining table. Trouble is, once you've built a beautiful one, your old chairs will look shabby in comparison. That's why we added seating to this special collection of favorite furniture projects from the pages of *Fine Woodworking* magazine.

Imagine a gorgeous dining table, like Mike Pekovich's classic Arts and Crafts hayrake design. Now surround it with Kevin Rodel's stately chairs in a similar style. That's the dream. Now go make it happen.

—Asa Christiana
Editor, *Fine Woodworking*

Make a Limbert-Style Coffee Table

GREGORY PAOLINI

There are many well-known designers of Arts and Crafts furniture, such as the Stickleys and the Greenes. But a lesser-known designer, Charles Limbert, has always held a special appeal for me. I'm especially fond of his oval library table. That's why I jumped at the chance to design and make a scaled-down version, to be used as a coffee table.

I've preserved the elliptical top and shelf, the gently curved legs, the decorative piercings in the stretchers, and Limbert's choice of wood—quartersawn white oak. I kept the overall proportions as well, so the parts come together just as harmoniously as they do in the original table.

A variety of joints are used. Bridle joints hold the legs and aprons together, and a half-lap joint is used where the stretchers and aprons intersect. The legs and shelf are

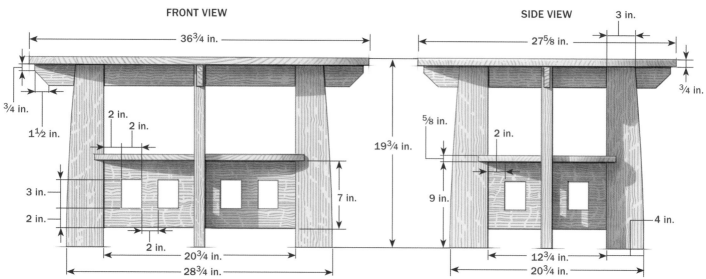

FRONT VIEW

36¾ in.

¾ in.

1½ in.

2 in.

2 in.

3 in.

2 in.

2 in.

20¾ in.

28¾ in.

19¾ in.

7 in.

SIDE VIEW

3 in.

27⅝ in.

¾ in.

⅝ in.

2 in.

9 in.

4 in.

12¾ in.

20¾ in.

notched where they meet, and slip tenons join the stretchers to the legs. Some of those joints can be tricky, but I'll show you some techniques to help you get flawless results. I'll also show you how to draw an accurate ellipse to take the mystery out of the top and shelf.

Pattern-rout the top and shelf

Begin by gluing up panels for the top and shelf and milling all of the parts. Then make full-size patterns for them. You'll need to draw two ellipses, which is easy to do with string, a pencil, and two small nails. To begin, draw the ellipse's axes on a piece of plywood 1 in. longer and wider than the ellipse and mark its length and width. Next, locate the foci, drive a nail into each focus, and tie a loop of string around the nails. When you stretch out the loop, it should just reach the side of the ellipse (see the drawing on p. 6). Put a pencil inside the loop and draw, keeping the string taut.

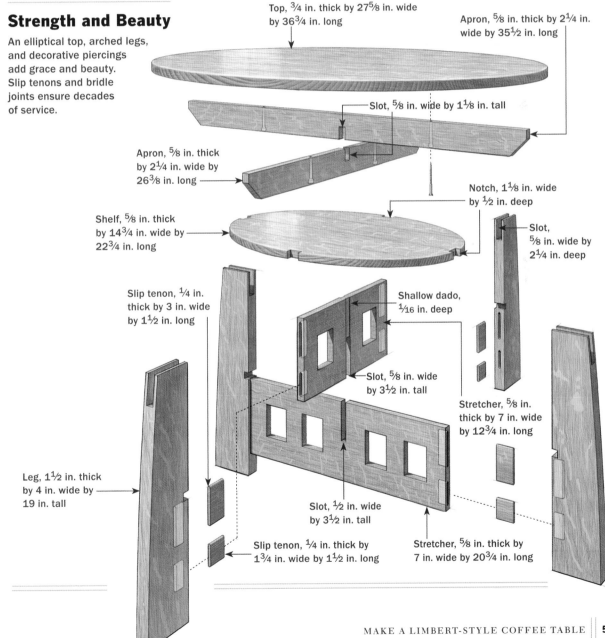

Strength and Beauty

An elliptical top, arched legs, and decorative piercings add grace and beauty. Slip tenons and bridle joints ensure decades of service.

Top, ¾ in. thick by 27⅝ in. wide by 36¾ in. long

Apron, ⅝ in. thick by 2¼ in. wide by 35½ in. long

Slot, ⅝ in. wide by 1⅛ in. tall

Apron, ⅝ in. thick by 2¼ in. wide by 26⅜ in. long

Notch, 1⅛ in. wide by ½ in. deep

Shelf, ⅝ in. thick by 14¾ in. wide by 22¾ in. long

Slot, ⅝ in. wide by 2¼ in. deep

Slip tenon, ¼ in. thick by 3 in. wide by 1½ in. long

Shallow dado, 1/16 in. deep

Slot, ⅝ in. wide by 3½ in. tall

Stretcher, ⅝ in. thick by 7 in. wide by 12¾ in. long

Leg, 1½ in. thick by 4 in. wide by 19 in. tall

Slot, ½ in. wide by 3½ in. tall

Slip tenon, ¼ in. thick by 1¾ in. wide by 1½ in. long

Stretcher, ⅝ in. thick by 7 in. wide by 20¾ in. long

How to Make a Perfect Ellipse

Both the top and shelf are elliptical. You can use a simple nail-and-string technique to make patterns for these. Each pattern does double duty. First, it lays out a line to follow at the bandsaw. And after the shape has been roughed out, the pattern serves as a template for a bushing-guided router.

Nails and string. Driven into the focal points, nails guide the string loop, which in turn guides the pencil along the perimeter of an ellipse.

KEY DIMENSIONS
Here's how to lay out the nails and size the string for each ellipse:

Top: $x = 13^{13}/_{16}$, $y = 24^1/_4$
Shelf: $x = 7^3/_8$, $y = 17^{15}/_{16}$

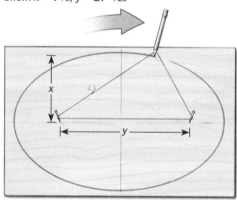

Simple, accurate ellipses. Size the string so the pencil reaches the x dimension (see drawing at left). Then keep the string taut as you trace an ellipse.

Cut the pattern at the bandsaw. Cut just outside the line, so there is less waste to remove when smoothing the curves.

With both ellipses drawn, cut them out at the bandsaw. Use 100-grit (CAMI) sandpaper, glued to a thin strip of wood, to remove the sawmarks and fair the curves. Then trace the patterns on the panels for the top and shelf. Before cutting out the top and shelf, cut the notches in the shelf that join it to the legs. This is far easier to do now, when the sides and ends are square, than after cutting the shelf into an ellipse. Lay out the notches by placing the legs on the shelf and transferring their thickness onto it. Then cut them at the tablesaw, using a crosscut sled. The width of the notches is critical, so cut the notch sides first and then nibble away

Notch the shelf before cutting the ellipse.
Because its width is critical, cut each side of
the notch first and then remove the middle. Use
stop blocks on your crosscut sled to ensure that
notches on opposite sides will line up.

Cut the top and shelf at the bandsaw. Use the patterns to trace
the shapes. When bandsawing, leave about ⅛ in. of waste for the
next step: routing the edges flush to your template.

If you try to rout the whole circle in one pass, you'll
tear out the grain in some areas, so you'll need to flip the
workpiece. Use a double-bearing, flush-trimming bit so there's
no need to change bits or reattach the template on the other
side. Just adjust the bit height to use the other bearing.

Always Rout Downhill

1. Rout two quarters with the template up.

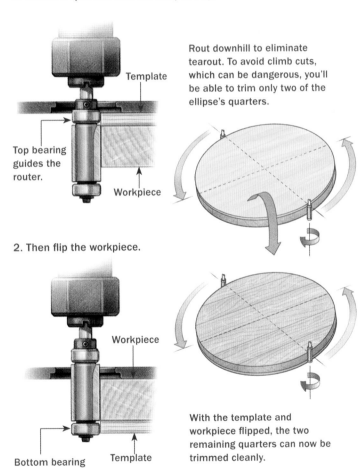

Rout downhill to eliminate
tearout. To avoid climb cuts,
which can be dangerous, you'll
be able to trim only two of the
ellipse's quarters.

Template

Top bearing
guides the
router.

Workpiece

2. Then flip the workpiece.

Workpiece

Bottom bearing
guides the router.

Template

With the template and
workpiece flipped, the two
remaining quarters can now be
trimmed cleanly.

the inside. Cut the notches a bit tight and fit
them with a chisel later.

After all four notches have been cut, head
to the bandsaw and cut out the elliptical top
and shelf. The top is heavy and unwieldy, so
cut away the bulk of each corner first. Then
make a second pass close to the line. I use a
flush-trimming bit to rout the top and shelf
flush to their patterns (see the photos above).

Join legs and aprons

With the top and shelf done, you can get
started on the joinery. The stretchers are
joined to the legs with slip tenons. Because

A lesson in bridle joints and slip tenons. Other than the mortises and slip tenons holding the stretchers to the legs, every joint in this table is some type of bridle joint or half-lap joint. A router makes quick work of the mortises, and a tablesaw, equipped with a standard combination blade, is the right tool for the bridle joints and half-laps. To rout mortises in the legs (shown), use a spiral bit that matches the mortise's width and use a fence on both sides of the router. Set up the router's edge guide and then clamp on a simple shopmade fence. The mating mortises in the stretchers are done the same way.

Fence and guide block keep the mortise on line. The mortise will be straight and parallel to the sides because the fence and guide block prevent the router from wandering.

the stretchers are 7 in. wide and could expand as much as $\frac{1}{16}$ in., break the mortise into two. The tenon will fit tightly in the upper mortise but loosely in the lower one, forcing the stretcher's movement downward and away from the shelf. I make the slip tenons by milling some white oak to the correct thickness and width, rounding over the edges at the router table, and then crosscutting the tenons to length. Now cut a notch in each leg. Paired with the notches in the shelf, they form a strong joint that holds the shelf in place and prevents the base from twisting or racking. Cut them just as you did the notches in the shelf. While you're at the tablesaw, go ahead and cut the slot for the bridle joint into the top of each leg. I use a tenoning jig, starting at the center of the slot

Bridle joints must be centered. Using a tenoning jig for the slot, cut in the middle of the leg first. Then flip the leg side to side to make the subsequent cuts.

Cut the curve last. After tracing the shape onto the leg, cut away the waste on the bandsaw and then clean up the sawmarks with a handplane or sander.

Slot the aprons and test the fit. After marking the joint, cut each side first and then nibble away the waste one pass at a time (far left). Cut the slots a bit tight at first and then sneak up on a tight joint, checking the fit after each trimming cut (left).

and working outward. As you get close to the sides of the slot, use the apron to test the fit.

A half-lap joint is used to connect the aprons where they intersect. For this joint, I cut a slot halfway through each apron. Unlike the notches in the legs and shelf, which were cut from the sides in, cut this joint from the center out. That will keep the joint centered on the aprons.

To complete the legs, cut the curve on the outside edge. I made a pattern out of ¼-in.-thick plywood and traced it on the legs. Save the offcuts to use as cauls during glue-up.

Slot and rout the stretchers

As with the aprons, a half-lap joint is used where the stretchers intersect. However, cut a shallow dado on both sides of the shorter stretcher to conceal the joint and reinforce it against racking.

After cutting the dadoes, raise the blade and cut a slot on the bottom edge of the stretcher. You won't be able to get the full depth with a 10-in. sawblade, so cut as deep as you can and finish up the slot with a handsaw and chisel. With the short stretcher done, cut the slot in the longer stretcher.

Now it's time to rout mortises in the ends of the stretchers to accept the slip tenons that join them to the legs. Do this the same way you routed the mortises in the legs, with a router and spiral bit.

After routing the mortises, use a template, plunge router, guide bushing, and spiral

Cut the dado with a standard-kerf blade. That way you can sneak up on the final width, testing how well the long stretcher fits into it as you go.

Start the slot at the tablesaw. With the blade as high as possible, cut the sides to line up with the dado, and nibble away the waste in between.

Go deeper with a handsaw. Follow the sides of the slot with the saw and then remove the rest of the waste with a chisel.

Use a Router Template for Clean Cutouts

There are six rectangular piercings. Use a router and template to make them all the same. A spiral bit is best because its shearing action will cut the end-grain areas smoothly.

Make the template at the router table. The author routs one side of the opening at a time, lowering the template onto a 1/4-in.-dia. spiral bit. He stops the last cut about 1/2 in. before the end and finishes it with a handsaw and sandpaper.

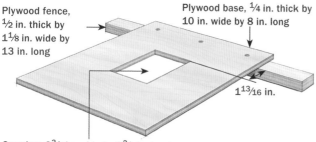

Plywood fence, 1/2 in. thick by 1 1/8 in. wide by 13 in. long

Plywood base, 1/4 in. thick by 10 in. wide by 8 in. long

1 13/16 in.

Opening, 3 3/8 in. wide by 2 3/8 in. long, includes offset for guide bushing

bit to rout the decorative piercings in the stretchers. Make the template from a piece of plywood and lay out the piercing on it, taking the bushing's offset into account. Head to the router table and cut out the opening. Attach a fence to the bottom side, lay out the location of the piercings on the stretchers, and you're ready to rout the openings.

Hog out most of the waste with a Forstner bit at the drill press. With most of the waste removed, clamp the template to the stretcher and the stretcher to the bench. Make a clockwise pass around the opening, increase the bit's depth, and make a second pass. Make a third pass to complete the piercing.

Dry-fit, stain, and glue-up

This little table is kind of like a puzzle, in that there are pieces that interlock and must be assembled in a particular order for the table to come together. Dry-fitting the table will help you not only learn and get comfortable with that puzzle but also find any joints that need to be tweaked.

Begin by putting the stretchers together and adding one leg. Fit the shelf into that leg and add the opposite leg. Then add the last two legs. Now add the aprons and put the top in place. Before you take the table apart, use a pencil to mark the joint where the aprons

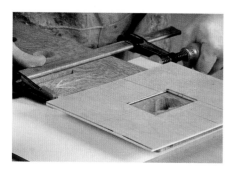

Remove most of the waste in the cutout. Then clamp the template to the stretcher. Place scrap beneath to protect your bench.

Trim flush in three passes. Set the bit depth to 1/4 in. for the first pass, 1/2 in. for the second, and 5/8 in. on the last one.

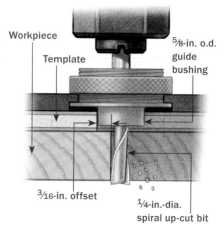

Workpiece

Template

5/8-in. o.d. guide bushing

3/16-in. offset

1/4-in.-dia. spiral up-cut bit

A dry run sorts out surprises. Start with the stretchers. As the core of the table, these should fit snugly and squarely.

Fit the slip tenons. Leave the bottom tenon narrow for wood movement.

The shelf is next. Lock it in place with opposing legs, then add the last two. If you assemble the legs first, you won't be able to get the shelf in place.

intersect and where they pass through the legs. The marks will remind you not to sand those areas, which would cause the joints to become loose. Also, as you take off the legs, number the inside of the notches—I use a felt-tipped marker—and number the corresponding legs to match. Numbering the aprons on the top edge is also a good idea.

After disassembling the table, break the edges with a block plane and then use a random-orbit sander to sand all of the parts up to P180-grit. Do not sand the areas you marked earlier: the half-lap joint where the aprons intersect and the area where the aprons pass through the bridle joint in the legs. Next, wipe all of the parts with a damp rag to raise the grain, then use a sanding block and P220-grit paper to remove the raised grain.

I finish the table before the glue-up. The advantage of finishing first is that any glue squeeze-out will not soak into the grain and become a problem when you try to finish over it. And squeeze-out doesn't stick to the finish, so it just peels away without fuss. To stain the table, I applied an antique cherry aniline dye. I let it dry overnight and then applied a dark walnut oil-based pigment stain. I finished it off with Minwax® Polycrylic water-based polyurethane. Tape off any area where glue will be applied, like the bridle and half-lap

joints on the aprons, and use caution when staining around them and the slots.

Now you're ready for the glue. You can do it in stages or, if you're feeling lucky, all at once. Repeat the assembly order from the dry-fitting and use the leg cutoffs as cauls for the clamps. After the glue is dry, peel away any squeeze-out. Then rub out the finish with 0000 steel wool and paste wax, and buff the wax with a shoe-shine cloth or brush. Finally, attach the top with four screws, driving through the aprons and into the top. Slot the holes on the short apron to allow for wood movement.

Aprons are the last piece to the puzzle. They hold the legs in place and make the base rigid.

Coffee Table in Mahogany

MARIO RODRIGUEZ

New York City's Lower East Side is an area often credited with cutting-edge trends in fashion, food, and home decor. Visit any specialty furniture shop there and you'll likely find some good examples of modern solid-wood Scandinavian furniture from the 1950s. Resurrected mostly from garages and attics, this furniture has a style that appeals to a fast-paced crowd that likes pieces with bold, vigorous lines and a clean, uncluttered look.

This table incorporates much of what's good about furniture from the post–World War II era. A thin top appears to hover above two muscular arching leg frames that look ready to stride across the room. At the bottom, the outside surface of each leg is shaped to create an edge at the center that looks much like a crease. As the crease extends higher on the leg, it gradually morphs into a smooth radius. It's an interesting detail, and one that's not easily lost on the eye.

Mill the material, then make the legs first

I used 8/4 stock for the legs and the leg rails of the table, and 4/4 stock for the stretchers,

the top, and the breadboard ends. Mahogany is a good choice for this project. It's readily available in long, wide boards; it works easily with both hand tools and machine tools; it sands smoothly; and it takes a finish well. Plus the patina improves with age. Indeed, it has been just over a year since I finished the table and it already has acquired a deep, coppery color.

I milled the stock to its final thickness: 1¾ in. thick for the legs and the leg rails, and ¾ in. thick for the stretchers, the top, and the breadboard ends. Then I cut the stretchers and the leg rails to width and length. Each leg starts at the floor as a slender, pointed foot. As it curves upward and disappears under the top, the edge of the leg flattens out to a smooth, robust curve.

Use a template to draw the legs

Begin work on the legs by making a template that matches the curve of the leg when viewed from the side (see the "The Overall Profile" on p. 14). Rather than draw the entire outside arc of the leg on the template, leave a little extra wood in the form of a "horn" at the top of each leg. This horn will provide a parallel surface so later, when it's time to clamp the leg and the leg rail assemblies, you can apply plenty of clamping pressure to ensure a tight joint. The horns will be cut off after the legs have been assembled to the top rails.

For each leg, you need stock that's 1¾ in. thick by 6 in. wide by 16 in. long. At least one of the corners must be square. Place the template on the stock, taking care to align the top and the inside edges with a square corner on the stock. Trace the outline with a pencil, then cut it out on a bandsaw, staying just slightly on the waste side of the marked line.

I cut the leg mortises before the tenons. That way, if the mortises end up oversize or undersize, the tenons can be adjusted as

Joinery for a Sturdy Table

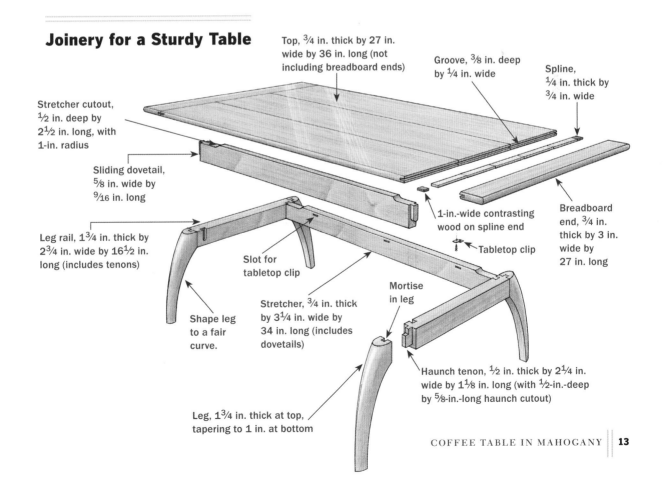

Top, ¾ in. thick by 27 in. wide by 36 in. long (not including breadboard ends)

Groove, ⅜ in. deep by ¼ in. wide

Spline, ¼ in. thick by ¾ in. wide

Stretcher cutout, ½ in. deep by 2½ in. long, with 1-in. radius

Sliding dovetail, ⅝ in. wide by 9/16 in. long

1-in.-wide contrasting wood on spline end

Breadboard end, ¾ in. thick by 3 in. wide by 27 in. long

Leg rail, 1¾ in. thick by 2¾ in. wide by 16½ in. long (includes tenons)

Slot for tabletop clip

Tabletop clip

Shape leg to a fair curve.

Stretcher, ¾ in. thick by 3¼ in. wide by 34 in. long (includes dovetails)

Mortise in leg

Haunch tenon, ½ in. thick by 2¼ in. wide by 1⅛ in. long (with ½-in.-deep by ⅝-in.-long haunch cutout)

Leg, 1¾ in. thick at top, tapering to 1 in. at bottom

The Overall Profile

Use a template to trace the shape of the leg (including a temporary horn), then bandsaw the profile and cut the leg mortises. Setting a photocopier to 200% will produce a full-size copy of the leg.

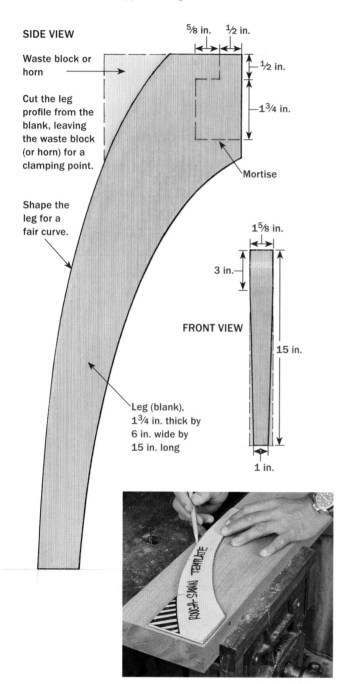

SIDE VIEW

5/8 in.   1/2 in.

Waste block or horn

1/2 in.

1 3/4 in.

Cut the leg profile from the blank, leaving the waste block (or horn) for a clamping point.

Mortise

Shape the leg for a fair curve.

FRONT VIEW

1 5/8 in.

3 in.

15 in.

Leg (blank), 1 3/4 in. thick by 6 in. wide by 15 in. long

1 in.

Do some shaping before assembly. Use a template to trace the leg profile. Duplicating the legs is much more uniform with a template.

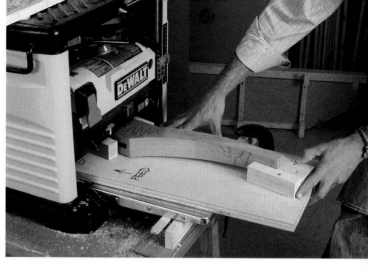

A thickness planer and two jigs are used to taper the sides of the legs. With a leg in one of the jigs, taper the first side by elevating the bottom end of the leg 3/8 in. (see the drawing on the facing page). Then transfer the leg to the second jig and taper the second side by raising the leg 3/4 in.

needed for a snug fit. Lay out the mortises with a marking gauge, positioning them exactly on center. The mortises can be cut easily enough with a drill and chisel. But I'm fortunate to have a mortiser, so I immediately put it to good use. To make the mortises at the right angle, I rest the horns on a block on the mortiser table.

Taper the leg

The leg taper is next. Each taper starts at a point 3 in. below the top and extends to the bottom of the leg. At the starting point, the leg has the full 1 3/4-in. width; then it tapers 3/8 in. on each side to produce a thickness of 1 in. at the bottom.

I use a thickness planer and a couple of simple jigs to create the tapers (see "Taper the Legs" on the facing page). Each jig is a rectangular base piece made of 3/4-in.-thick plywood. The leg blank is placed on the base, roughly perpendicular to the planer cutterhead. Then a few wood blocks are butted up to the blank to hold it in position as it travels through the planer. The first jig has a spacer that raises the end 3/8 in. above the base. The second jig, which is a mirror image of the first, has a spacer that raises the opposite face of the leg a total of 3/4 in.

If you'd rather not make the jigs or use a planer for the tapers, you can scribe the tapers along the edge of each leg and then use a bandsaw to trim away most of the waste. A couple of lengths of masking tape work just fine as straightedges that easily conform to the curve of the leg. After bandsawing, complete the taper by using a handplane to smooth the sides of each leg right up to the scribed lines.

Make the leg rails and assemble the legs

With the leg tapers completed, work on the two leg rails. Each one needs tenons on both ends and a pair of dovetail mortises on the inside face. A haunched tenon is a good choice. The haunch provides added glue surface without weakening the tops of the legs.

Use a marking gauge to lay out the tenon thickness. Then, with a tablesaw and miter gauge, make a cut along both sides and the bottom edge to create the shoulders. After that, use the tablesaw to make the first haunch cut. Following the layout lines, cut the cheeks a little fat on the bandsaw. Make two more cuts at the bandsaw, one to complete the haunch and one to trim the tenon to width. Finally, use a fine rasp or

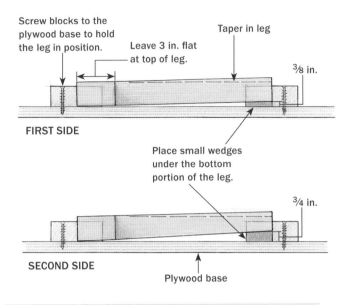

Taper the Legs

Screw blocks to the plywood base to hold the leg in position.

Taper in leg

Leave 3 in. flat at top of leg.

³⁄₈ in.

FIRST SIDE

Place small wedges under the bottom portion of the leg.

³⁄₄ in.

SECOND SIDE

Plywood base

shoulder plane to thin the cheeks as needed for a perfect fit in the mating leg mortise.

The dovetail mortises for the leg rails are cut with a router and a ³⁄₄-in., 7° router bit. I stop the dovetail mortises ½ in. short of the bottom edge of the rail. A pencil mark on the router table tells me when to stop.

Each leg frame is made up of two legs and a leg rail. With the horns still attached to

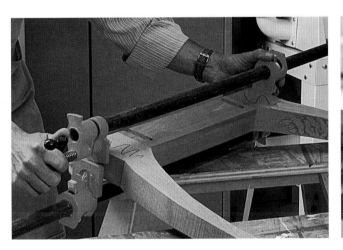

Assemble the leg frames. Cut the dovetail grooves in the leg rails, then join the leg rails to the legs (left). The horns prove handy here, as they provide purchase for the clamp jaws. Trim the horns after the glue dries (right).

Fair the leg curves and mark the centerline. The bandsaw leaves the legs with a rough surface, so the author starts the shaping process by smoothing the front of each leg and marking a centerline (shown), with a strip of tape serving as a flexible straightedge.

Track Your Progress with Profile Gauges

Like the hull of a schooner, the cross-sectional profile of the leg changes along its length, so it helps to make a few gauges (photocopy the sketches at 100% to make the patterns) that can be used to check progress.

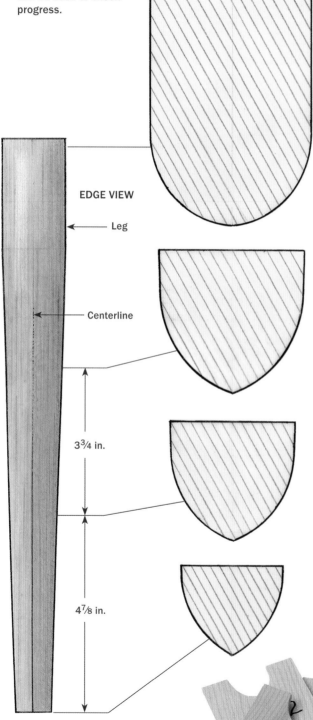

EDGE VIEW

Leg

Centerline

3¾ in.

4⅞ in.

the legs, you should be able to glue up each frame with a couple of clamps. Before gluing, though, give the underside of the legs and the rails a thorough sanding. After gluing up, check the flatness of the frames with a straightedge. Clean up excess glue with a damp rag, then set the frames aside to dry.

Now finish shaping the legs

After removing the clamps, return to the bandsaw to cut away the horns. Now it's time to finish sculpting the legs. There are two objectives at this point: The first is to shape the outline to a smooth arc with no blips, depressions, or flat spots. The second is to shape the changing profile of the leg.

I use a spokeshave to shape the arc of the leg into a smooth curve. Adjust the spokeshave to produce thick curls for the heaviest cuts, then readjust the blade for fine, gossamer shavings as the curve becomes more refined. A microplane (one of those stainless-steel cheese grater–type cutters) can be helpful here. It can be easier to use in situations in which the grain constantly changes.

Profile gauges. Make the simple gauges from thin plywood, and number them.

Start shaping the legs. Using a spokeshave, start profiling the leg (1). With the gauges in hand, periodically check the progress of the profile along the front edge of each leg (2). After the spokeshave has done much of the heavy lifting, a rasp is perfect for further smoothing the leg surfaces. Sand the leg with a block to get a smooth surface without rounding the center crease (3).

With the arc of the curve generally smooth, I use a piece of tape as a flexible rule to mark a line down the center and establish the crease. For the crease to really stand out, cut away material just to the sides of it. Otherwise the curve will flatten out, appearing fat and making the crease look soft.

To gauge progress, it helps to make a series of section templates to fit against the work as you shape the legs. Work away from the scribed line and the "knee," in the direction of the grain, being careful to leave a smooth surface with crisp corners. Once most of the material has been removed with a spokeshave, a wood rasp is perfect for adjusting the profile and shaping the razor-sharp crease in the front edge of the leg. The longer the rasp, the easier it will be to achieve a smooth curve.

For the final shaping and smoothing, a flat card scraper is indispensable. I reground the edge of my scraper to a subtle concave curve to better blend the changing contours of the leg.

Finally, use 100-grit sandpaper to remove tool marks, finish off the crease, and complete the shaping of the legs. I find 100-grit coarse enough to remove material

and make subtle changes in the shape but not so coarse that it takes hours of remedial sanding to remove leftover scratches. During this stage, I often wet the leg with denatured alcohol to highlight any tearout, tool marks, or rough spots that need to be removed before progressing to a finer grit.

Make the stretchers

The two stretchers connect the leg frames, forming the base of the table. Stretchers also provide a means to attach the tabletop to the base.

I put my router table to use again, this time cutting the dovetails on the stretcher ends. There's no need to do anything with the bit; it remains at the same height for this cut. This time, though, use an L-shaped fence clamped to the table to support the stretcher. A notch in the fence allows you to bury the bit. In addition, use a secondary fence to prevent the piece from tipping from front to back. Make a few trial cuts until the fit is perfect.

Cut a dovetail on the stretcher ends. The same router bit used earlier to cut dovetail grooves in the leg rails, set to the same height, cuts the dovetail on each end of the stretchers (left). Aim for a smooth, sliding fit. A rasp then shapes one end of the dovetail to fit the stopped dovetail groove in the leg rail (above).

Using a rasp, round over the bottom edge of the notch so it fits at the end of the dovetail mortise in the leg rail.

The top edge of each stretcher is cut away at the ends, producing the effect of a tabletop that floats above the leg frames. Begin by marking out the location of the cutout that creates the narrowed end. Cut it out on the bandsaw, staying just on the waste side of the line. Use a drum sander, then a scraper to smooth the sawn edge to the line.

After the leg frames have been sanded, apply glue to the stretcher dovetails and the dovetail mortises on the leg rails. Then assemble the stretchers and the leg frames, adding a couple of bar clamps to make sure everything stays in place until the glue has dried.

Using the router and a ⅛-in.-wide slot-cutting bit, cut four short grooves in each leg rail. Make them just long enough to accept small, metal tabletop clips on the inside surface of the rails.

Glue up the top and add the breadboard ends

After ripping the boards for the top to nearly equal width, and crosscutting each one a little on the long side, I join them with biscuits.

Once dry, I use a crosscut sled to square the ends of the assembled top on the tablesaw.

Breadboard ends give the table a clean look and help keep the top flat. The easiest way to mount the breadboard ends is to use a router with a ¼-in. slot-cutting bit and cut a groove on the inside edge of each breadboard and on the ends of the top. A solid-wood spline goes in the grooves. The top must be able to expand and contract with seasonal changes in humidity. To accommodate this movement, I glue the spline to the top along its entire width. On the breadboard end, I apply the glue at the midpoint for about 12 in. This is sufficient to keep the top flat and strong, yet allows it to move without cracking.

I use ¼-in.-thick mahogany stock for the spline, but any hardwood will work. In order for the spline to move in unison with the top, the grain of the spline must run parallel to

Install the stretchers. Once glue is applied to the mating surfaces, slip the stretcher dovetails into the leg-rail mortises. Add clamps to the assembly. A pair of clamps spanning the stretchers helps ensure a tight joint.

An easy technique for breadboard ends. A long mahogany spline, capped on each end with a short piece of walnut, is glued into a groove on each end of the top (above). On the breadboard-end groove, apply glue on only about 12 in. at the midpoint. A couple of pipe clamps apply pressure to the joint connecting the top and breadboard ends (right).

the grain of the top. The spline doesn't need to be one piece from one side of the top to the other. Several narrower pieces, placed side by side, work just as effectively. To create visual contrast, I add a short piece of walnut at each end of the spline. This is an eye-catching detail, so a clean, tight job is a must.

Once the top, the splines, and the breadboard ends are assembled, a couple of pipe clamps provide enough pressure on the joints.

Now, with the breadboard ends mounted, round over all the top edges using a ⅜-in. quarter-round bit on the router table. The result is a ¾-in. radius around all four edges of the top.

Next, place the base in the center of the upside-down tabletop. Slip the table-mounting clips into the slots cut earlier. Secure each clip to the underside of the top with a screw.

Apply finish to the table

I chose Waterlox® Original for the finish. It's easy to apply and can be rejuvenated without fuss. After sanding all surfaces with 220-grit sandpaper, brush on two coats within a couple of hours and allow the table to dry for 24 hours. Then sand with 220-grit sandpaper.

Mount the top and apply the finish. After attaching the top to the base, finish the table. A few coats of Waterlox Original, followed by a coat of paste wax, complete the project.

The result is a casual open-pore surface that's easy to maintain.

Adding more coats and wet sanding with Waterlox produces a smoother, high-gloss finish. Either approach gives great results.

The next step is to wipe on a light coat of Waterlox with a rag to brighten and even out the finish. As a final step, apply a coat of paste wax and buff all the surfaces to a soft luster.

Coffee Table Puts Joinery on Display

KEVIN RODEL

Arts and Crafts style is noteworthy for taking joinery—the product of the craftsman's hand—and elevating it to the level of artistic decoration. The basis of this table design is four decorative joints: through-tenons, grid work, half-lap joints, and breadboard ends. These design elements work beautifully together in tables of almost any size.

Although the project detailed here is a coffee table, the techniques are the same for all of the tables illustrated on p. 31. I usually build the base first. Start by milling the leg stock to the required square dimensions and then cut it to length.

Cut mortises before tenons

A rule of thumb is to cut mortises before cutting and fitting tenons. Lay out the mortises in the legs. The aprons are joined to the upper portion of each leg with stopped mortises, which intersect inside the leg. Keep in mind that the leg and apron junction is not flush; the apron is set back from the outside face of the leg, so lay out the mortises accordingly. I recommend a ¾-in. shoulder at the top of each mortise to keep the end grain from splitting, but only a ¼-in. shoulder is necessary at the bottom. Make the tenon ⅜ in. thick. All of these apron mortises can be done with the same machine setup, whether you are using a mortising machine or a plunge router.

The through-tenons at the lower end of each leg are thicker because they also function as a decorative detail. Note that the ends of the tenons are both beveled and wedged, in that order. Make each through-tenon about half the thickness of the leg stock and, of course, centered. That means a ⅞-in.-thick tenon for the 1¾-in.-thick leg on the coffee table. There is no need for a variety of cutting bits to make large mortises for these through-tenons. I make two cuts with a ½-in.-dia. bit, referencing off opposite sides of the leg, which guarantees the mortise is centered. When cutting a through-mortise, set the stops to cut a little more than halfway through the leg and then turn the workpiece around and finish cutting from the opposite face.

Because the tenon will receive two wedges when assembled, the mortise must be flared slightly toward its outer, visible face. To flare the mortise, simply add an extra ¹⁄₁₆ in. when laying out the upper and lower ends of the outer face. Then follow the layout lines when mortising halfway through from each side. Don't worry about the small step created inside each end of the mortise. The tenon will be made to fit snugly into the shorter inside length of the mortise, and the wedges will flare the tenon at the top and bottom to close the gap and leave a neat-looking joint.

A final, optional design detail is the small coves I add to the bottom of each leg. They

Harmonious details will work in tables of many sizes.

Beveled through-tenons

Grid-work stretcher

Breadboard ends with ebony accents

can be cut most easily on a router table with a bearing-guided ¼-in.-radius cove bit, but you also can use a laminate trimmer and a steady hand.

With the legs complete, make up the apron parts and tenon the ends. The tenons will intersect within the mortises, so cut the ends at a 45° angle.

On the arched stretchers, complete the joinery first

The most labor-intensive pieces in this design are the arched stretchers in the table base. The key is to complete the joinery before doing anything else.

When cutting the stock to length, remember that the through-tenons will protrude ⅜ in. beyond the legs. It is critical that a through-tenon fits snug in the mortise—not so tight that you need to force it in with a mallet or so loose that the joint will fall apart from its own weight. When satisfied with the fit, dry-assemble the joint and use a sharp pencil to mark around the tenon where it protrudes through the leg. This line will help you set up the tablesaw for cutting the bevels on the tenon ends. Use a good crosscut blade and don't cut right up to this line; leave ¹⁄₁₆ in. or so between the cut

Inside the Joinery

This Arts and Crafts coffee table is made of fumed or stained white oak. The two ends of the base—with their beveled and wedged through-tenons—are built first and then connected by the grid-work stretcher. The top receives breadboard ends with decorative ebony details.

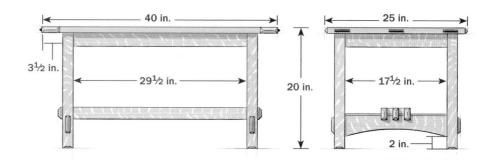

40 in.

25 in.

$3\frac{1}{2}$ in.

$29\frac{1}{2}$ in.

20 in.

$17\frac{1}{2}$ in.

2 in.

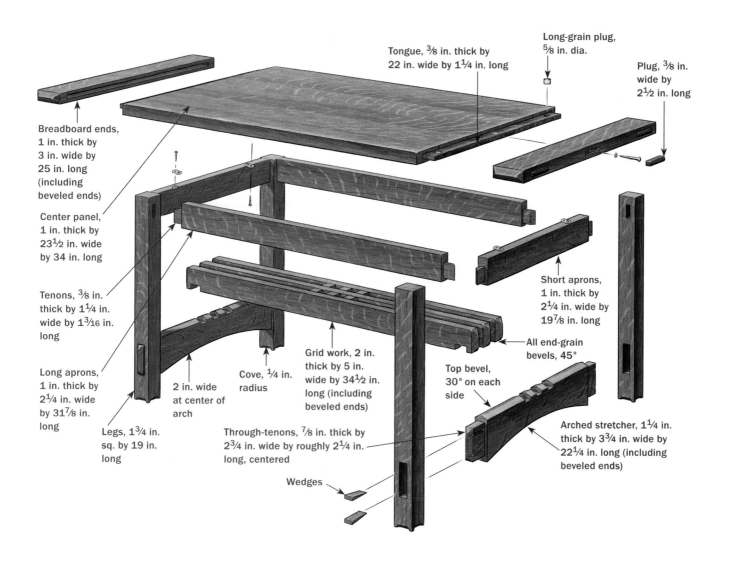

Tongue, $\frac{3}{8}$ in. thick by 22 in. wide by $1\frac{1}{4}$ in. long

Long-grain plug, $\frac{5}{8}$ in. dia.

Plug, $\frac{3}{8}$ in. wide by $2\frac{1}{2}$ in. long

Breadboard ends, 1 in. thick by 3 in. wide by 25 in. long (including beveled ends)

Center panel, 1 in. thick by $23\frac{1}{2}$ in. wide by 34 in. long

Tenons, $\frac{3}{8}$ in. thick by $1\frac{1}{4}$ in. wide by $1\frac{3}{16}$ in. long

Long aprons, 1 in. thick by $2\frac{1}{4}$ in. wide by $31\frac{7}{8}$ in. long

Legs, $1\frac{3}{4}$ in. sq. by 19 in. long

2 in. wide at center of arch

Cove, $\frac{1}{4}$ in. radius

Grid work, 2 in. thick by 5 in. wide by $34\frac{1}{2}$ in. long (including beveled ends)

Through-tenons, $\frac{7}{8}$ in. thick by $2\frac{3}{4}$ in. wide by roughly $2\frac{1}{4}$ in. long, centered

Wedges

Top bevel, 30° on each side

All end-grain bevels, 45°

Short aprons, 1 in. thick by $2\frac{1}{4}$ in. wide by $19\frac{7}{8}$ in. long

Arched stretcher, $1\frac{1}{4}$ in. thick by $3\frac{3}{4}$ in. wide by $22\frac{1}{4}$ in. long (including beveled ends)

and the pencil line. Now scrape, file, or sand the exposed end of the tenon. When the base is assembled, the beveled end should appear to grow right from the surface of the leg.

Before assembling the table base, bandsaw two kerfs in each tenon—almost down to the shoulder—to receive the wedges. Locate these kerfs about ⅜ in. from the ends and drill holes at the bottoms to keep the piece from splitting.

Notch the arched stretchers for the grid work

With the through-tenons complete, notch the arched stretchers for the half-lap joints to hold the grid work. The half-laps are not going to be flush; half of the thickness of the grid work sits atop the arched stretchers. Therefore, the depth of the notches in the arched stretchers as well as those in the underside of the grid work should be a quarter of the thickness of the grid work. Each member of the grid work is 1 in. wide and spaced 1 in. apart, dimensions that determine the width and spacing of the notches.

TIP Detailing the bottom of each leg is easier if done before assembling the legs and stretchers.

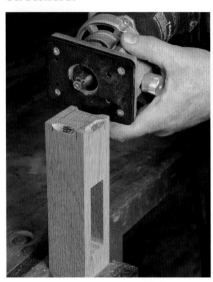

Dry-fit the joint and mark for the bevel cuts. Use a sharp pencil. Note that the outer portion of the mortise is the most critical: Be sure that its thickness fits the through-tenon exactly and that there is extra width to allow for the wedging action.

Bevel the tenons on the tablesaw. Undercut the bevels by about 1/16 in. Trim them to fit with a file and a sanding block.

Prepare the tenons for the wedges. Use the bandsaw to cut a kerf at each end and drill holes at the bottom of the kerfs to keep the workpiece from splitting.

I cut the notches in a series of passes with a fine crosscut blade on the tablesaw, using a crosscut sled and working to the layout lines. In keeping with the beveled look used throughout the piece, I also bevel the top edge of the arched stretchers 30° on each side, so it comes to a point.

To make the arch, use a shopmade template of ¼-in.-thick material several inches longer than the stretcher. Lay out, cut, and smooth a curve that is pleasing to your eye. Use the template to lay out the stretchers, and bandsaw them close to the line. Then attach the template to each stretcher with double-faced tape and use a bearing-guided, flush-cutting router bit to smooth the arch.

Assemble the ends of the base

At this point, finish sanding all of the parts made so far and assemble the ends of the table base. Before glue-up, make two wedges for each through-tenon. The wedges should be thick enough to fill the ¹⁄₁₆-in. gap at each end of the mortise before they bottom out in the sawkerf.

Drive and trim the wedges. During glue-up, drive in the two wedges evenly to ensure proper assembly (above). After the glue has set, use a chisel to trim the wedges flush with the beveled ends (below). Use sandpaper to clean up the surface, including any glue residue.

Before assembly, notch the stretchers. Use the tablesaw to notch the arched stretchers for the grid work. For uniform results, use the same fence and stop setup for the two outside notches.

Grid Work Looks Harder Than It Is

The grid work introduces another geometric element to the angular feel of this design. Like the other end-grain areas of the table, the ends of the grid work are beveled. Half-lap joints connect the grid-work stretcher to the arched stretchers.

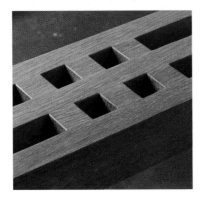

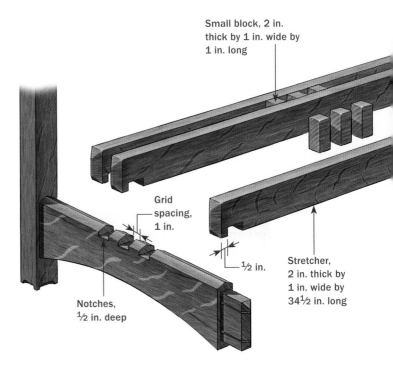

Small block, 2 in. thick by 1 in. wide by 1 in. long

Grid spacing, 1 in.

½ in.

Stretcher, 2 in. thick by 1 in. wide by 34½ in. long

Notches, ½ in. deep

When gluing the through-mortises and tenons, I have found it best to apply glue on the tenon only. Spread the glue so that it does not get onto the exposed end and also leaves bare the inner third of the cheek, next to the shoulder. As you seat the tenon in the mortise, the glue will spread backward and cover the entire tenon surface, ideally without oozing out at the shoulder. Never apply glue in a through-mortise; it only will push out onto the tenon end and the leg, leaving a mess that is hard to clean up and that might interfere with the finish.

Glue-up of this subassembly should be organized and quick. As soon as the two legs, apron, and arched stretcher are in clamps and checked for square—but before the glue has set—apply a small amount of glue to the ends of the wedges and drive them into the sawkerfs with a small hammer. Do one tenon and then the other, but alternate hammer

Fit the pieces to the notches. When milling the pieces for the grid work, test-fit them in the half-lap notches in the arched stretchers.

blows to the wedges of any one tenon so that both wedges go in equally. Saw off most of the excess with a dovetail saw and then pare the surface clean with a chisel.

Build and attach the grid work

With each end of the table base complete, dry-fit the entire base using the long apron members. Be sure that the tenons in the apron don't hit each other inside the legs.

Now it's time to decide exactly how long to make the grid work. It should protrude at least 1 in. beyond the arched stretchers; otherwise, the half-lap joints may be weak. Once you have settled on the length, mill three pieces of stock to the required width, 1 in., but leave them about ¼ in. thicker than

The grid work is simply blocks and butt joints. To make the glue-up manageable, start by joining just two of the long grid parts with three small blocks. Place waxed paper under the assembly and press it down as you clamp it. After the glue has begun to set, add the last stick and blocks to the assembly.

TIP A combination square will ensure that the grid work remains square during glue-up.

the final dimension and at least 3 in. longer. Test-fit these pieces in the half-lap notches you cut earlier in the arched stretchers.

From the excess length, cut off enough 1-in.-long blocks to form the grid, leaving a few extra as temporary spacers. Now cut the three long pieces to their exact length and bevel the ends on the tablesaw just as you did the ends of the through-tenons. Be sure to keep these three pieces the same length. Then, on a flat surface, clamp them together, ends square. Find the centerline and use a sharp pencil to lay out the grid.

The grid work appears complicated but is actually built with simple butt joints between the long and the short pieces.

Dry-fit the grid work to lay out its notches

When the grid work is assembled and the glue is set, send the assembly through the planer on each side, taking light cuts to bring it down to final thickness and to level out any inconsistencies in the grid. Now place the assembly on the base and fit it into the half-

Mark the grid work for its lap joints. After lightly planing the whole assembly, set it in the stretcher notches and scribe its mating half-lap joints.

Notch the grid work on the tablesaw. Insert filler blocks between the long parts of the grid to keep them from flexing during the process.

lap notches. With a knife, scribe the location of the half-laps to be cut into the underside of the grid work. At this point, the extra 1-in. spacer blocks come into play. Tape or hold them in place several inches away from each end to keep the parts from flexing while you cut the half-lap notches on the tablesaw.

To finish assembling the table base, first glue and clamp the end assemblies to the remaining apron members and then attach the grid work. Rather than trusting glue alone to secure the half-lap joints, I like the additional security of screwing these members together from below.

Make the breadboard ends

With the top panel glued up and surfaced, you are ready to make the breadboard joints. Consider the anatomy of the breadboard ends when cutting the top to length (see "Cap off the Top with Breadboard Ends" below), remembering to allow for the two tongues. I make the breadboard tongues 1¼ in. long.

Now, scribe the shoulder line for the tongue around all sides. I attach the finished breadboard with screws driven through its edges into the end grain of the tabletop. However, a screw in end grain does not provide the strongest joint without some modification, so before cutting the tongue, I glue wood plugs into the end grain to give the screws some long grain to bite into. While the plugs are drying, make up the breadboards. In keeping with the overall aesthetics of the piece, I purposely make the breadboards longer than the table width and bevel their end grain to match the ends of the through-tenons in the base. Be sure the length of the breadboards is sufficient to withstand seasonal wood movement; they should remain a little longer than the width of the tabletop, even when it expands due to humidity.

Center the long mortise in the breadboard and cut it a little deeper than the 1¼-in.-long tongue will be. Stop this slot about 1 in. from each end. The center of each breadboard is

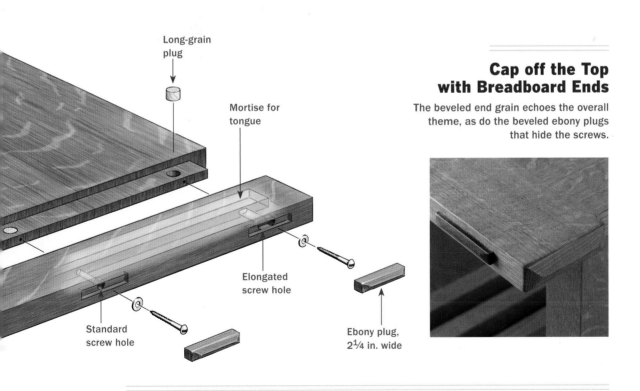

Long-grain plug

Mortise for tongue

Elongated screw hole

Standard screw hole

Ebony plug, 2¼ in. wide

Cap off the Top with Breadboard Ends

The beveled end grain echoes the overall theme, as do the beveled ebony plugs that hide the screws.

Fit the ends over the tabletop tongue. Mortise the breadboards first, then cut and fit the tongues.

Cap the screw holes with ebony plugs. Elongate the two screw holes at the ends of the breadboard to allow the tabletop to shrink and expand.

TIP Plugs driven into the ends of the tabletop provide a better grip for the screws than end grain.

attached with a screw and glue, while the end screws pass through slotted holes and are used without glue. On the opposite edge of each breadboard, where the ebony plugs will be located, make ¼-in.-deep slots, ⅜ in. wide, squaring the ends with a chisel. Use a drill press to drill clearance holes through the center of these shallow slots. Elongate the outside holes to allow for wood movement.

Now, back to the tongue. Using a plunge router and a breadboard-end jig, cut the tongue to its ⅜-in. thickness. Trim the ends of each tongue to allow for seasonal expansion, and dry-fit the breadboard to be sure of a snug fit.

Next, insert an awl through the screw holes to mark on the tongue's end grain where the screws will enter. If you did everything right, these points will line up with the hardwood plugs in the tongue. Remove the breadboard, drill pilot holes for the screws, add glue to only the center few inches of the joint, reattach the breadboard, and drive all of the screws.

Finally, make up some ebony (or any other dark wood) plugs to cover the slots and screw heads. After finish-sanding or scraping the top, attach it to the base. I used white oak for this project and darkened it with ammonia fumes. I finish all of my work with Tried & True™ linseed-oil finishes, which have a tone that warms up the cool color of fumed white oak.

One Design, Many Tables

My goal as a furniture maker always has been to develop a design vocabulary, which in turn would allow me to create a line of furniture incorporating pieces that work well together and seem to come from a single maker. This table design is no exception. By changing the dimensions of the stock, you can build similar tables: coffee table, end table/nightstand, sofa/hall table, or dining table. Combining these pieces in a home will unify the decor. The pieces are

The coffee table and end table work well together. Both share the same design details.

similar enough to create a nice theme, but they're different enough to avoid the feeling of boring repetition.

One key difference is the tabletops: A simple inlay is enough for the top of the end table, whereas the dining table has a tile inlay. Of course, for these designs to work visually, the thicknesses of some elements must be adjusted appropriately.

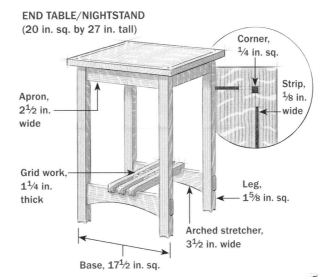

END TABLE/NIGHTSTAND
(20 in. sq. by 27 in. tall)

Corner, 1/4 in. sq.

Strip, 1/8 in. wide

Apron, 2 1/2 in. wide

Grid work, 1 1/4 in. thick

Leg, 1 5/8 in. sq.

Arched stretcher, 3 1/2 in. wide

Base, 17 1/2 in. sq.

The end table gets a simple inlay. Breadboards would be overkill for this small tabletop. The ebony inlay echoes the ebony plugs in the other table.

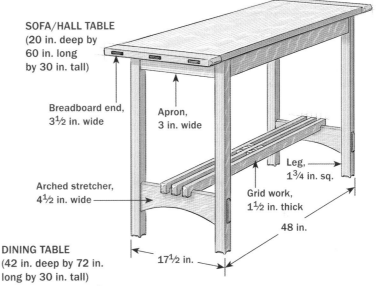

SOFA/HALL TABLE
(20 in. deep by 60 in. long by 30 in. tall)

Breadboard end, 3 1/2 in. wide

Apron, 3 in. wide

Arched stretcher, 4 1/2 in. wide

Leg, 1 3/4 in. sq.

Grid work, 1 1/2 in. thick

48 in.

17 1/2 in.

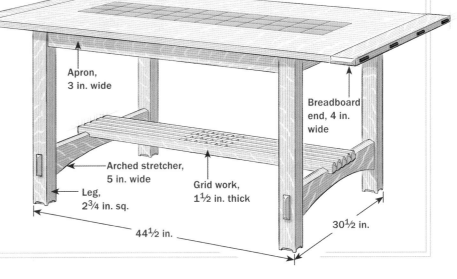

DINING TABLE
(42 in. deep by 72 in. long by 30 in. tall)

Apron, 3 in. wide

Breadboard end, 4 in. wide

Arched stretcher, 5 in. wide

Grid work, 1 1/2 in. thick

Leg, 2 3/4 in. sq.

44 1/2 in.

30 1/2 in.

Shaker Classic Two Ways

CHRISTIAN BECKSVOORT

Not long ago, a couple ordered a set of cherry side tables from me, one for each side of their pencil-post bed. I based the design on a Shaker side table from Canterbury, N.H., although virtually every other Shaker community had similar designs. As a surprise (I don't recommend this unless you are very familiar with your clients), I decided to make slightly different versions: one with square tapered legs, the other with turned tapered legs.

The overall design is a basic, timeless one that can move from bedroom to living room. But notice how the simple leg change alters the whole feel of the table. Tweaking the dimensions or shapes can make a big difference in the look of a piece of furniture. As far as difficulty goes, the table with tapered legs is a very good project to tackle if you're a beginner, and the one with turned legs adds a bit of a challenge. The rest of the construction is standard mortise-and-tenon

(continued on p. 36)

Side Table with Drawer

This little table design, taken from the Shakers, is rock solid, no matter which legs it stands on.

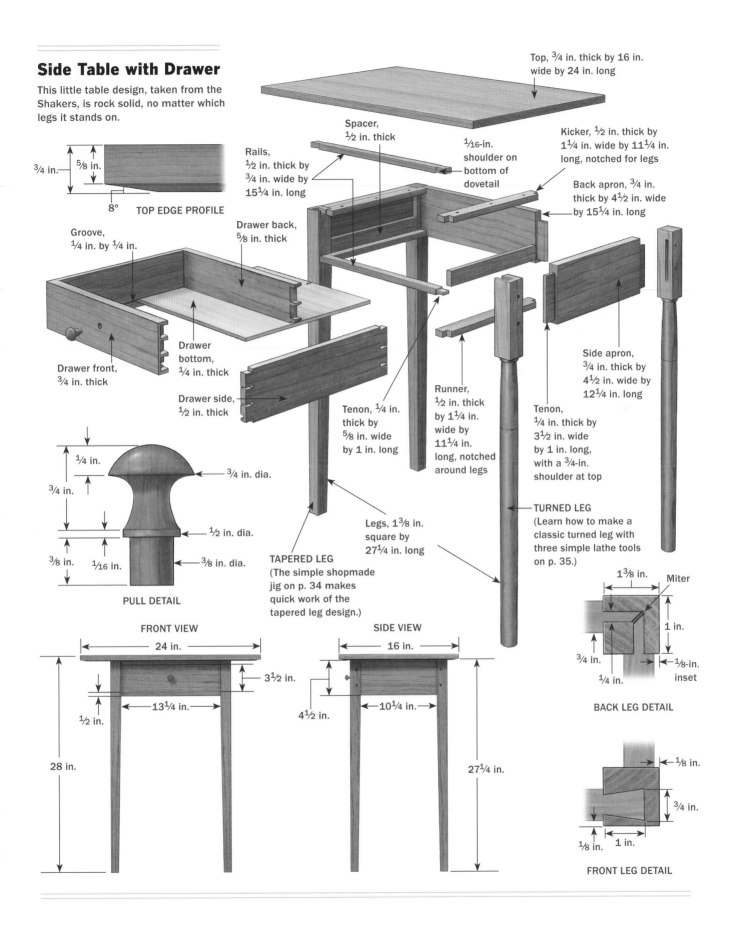

Top, ¾ in. thick by 16 in. wide by 24 in. long

Spacer, ½ in. thick

Rails, ½ in. thick by ¾ in. wide by 15¼ in. long

¹⁄₁₆-in. shoulder on bottom of dovetail

Kicker, ½ in. thick by 1¼ in. wide by 11¼ in. long, notched for legs

Back apron, ¾ in. thick by 4½ in. wide by 15¼ in. long

TOP EDGE PROFILE

¾ in.

⅝ in.

8°

Groove, ¼ in. by ¼ in.

Drawer back, ⅝ in. thick

Drawer bottom, ¼ in. thick

Drawer front, ¾ in. thick

Drawer side, ½ in. thick

Tenon, ¼ in. thick by ⅝ in. wide by 1 in. long

Runner, ½ in. thick by 1¼ in. wide by 11¼ in. long, notched around legs

Side apron, ¾ in. thick by 4½ in. wide by 12¼ in. long

Tenon, ¼ in. thick by 3½ in. wide by 1 in. long, with a ¾-in. shoulder at top

TURNED LEG
(Learn how to make a classic turned leg with three simple lathe tools on p. 35.)

PULL DETAIL

¼ in.

¾ in.

⅜ in.

¾ in. dia.

½ in. dia.

⅜ in. dia.

¹⁄₁₆ in.

Legs, 1⅜ in. square by 27¼ in. long

TAPERED LEG
(The simple shopmade jig on p. 34 makes quick work of the tapered leg design.)

FRONT VIEW

24 in.

3½ in.

13¼ in.

½ in.

28 in.

SIDE VIEW

16 in.

4½ in.

10¼ in.

27¼ in.

BACK LEG DETAIL

1⅜ in.

Miter

1 in.

¾ in.

¼ in.

⅛-in. inset

FRONT LEG DETAIL

⅛ in.

¾ in.

⅛ in.

1 in.

Two Options for Legs

When building tables, it's logical to start with the legs because they tie all the other parts together. Use a tapering jig on the tablesaw to taper the two inside faces or turn the round legs on the lathe.

The tapering jig to create these two-sided tapered legs is simple to make. Use a piece of plywood 4 in. to 6 in. wide and 3 in. to 4 in. longer than the leg. I mark the end of the leg to see the final dimensions and use those marks to position the leg on the plywood. Set the leg on the edge of the plywood with the portion to be tapered flush with the end and overhanging the edge. Then trace around the leg and cut the leg area away freehand on the bandsaw. Once that's done, screw that piece of plywood to a base piece and add hold-down clamps to keep the leg stock secure as you run it through the tablesaw.

After cutting the first taper, turn the leg 90° in the jig and cut the second one. The final step is cleaning up the tapers with a sander.

A Jig Makes Tapers Easy

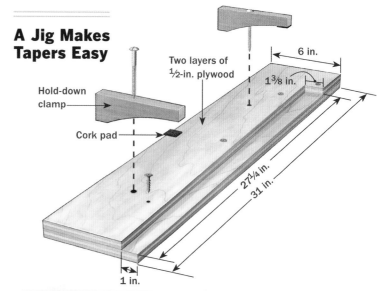

Hold-down clamp

Cork pad

Two layers of ½-in. plywood

6 in.

1⅜ in.

27¼ in.

31 in.

1 in.

TAPERED LEG

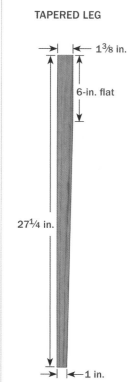

1⅜ in.

6-in. flat

27¼ in.

1 in.

Use a leg to lay out the jig. Then bandsaw the leg cutout on the top piece.

First taper. With the leg in the jig and the rip fence set to the width of the jig, rip the taper on the first inside face of the leg.

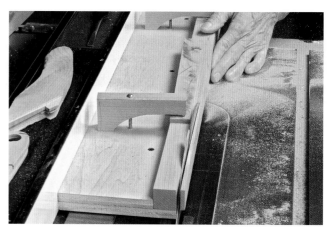

Second taper. Turn the leg blank 90° in the jig and cut the taper on the second inside face.

Although the turned legs aren't as easy as the tapered legs, the turning is pretty basic. There are a few points to keep in mind: the transition where the square top turns round, the ¼-in.-wide ring just under that, the maximum diameter, and the gentle taper down to the bottom of the leg.

Going from the square top portion to the round at a 90° angle is a little tricky because a false move can knock off the corners. If you're not too secure on the lathe, you can start with 1⅝-in.-square stock and size it to 1⅜ in. after turning to remove any tearout.

First, measure and mark the transition location on all four sides of the leg. Then begin turning with a ½-in. gouge as close to that point as possible. Next, with a diamond-point scraper held on edge, carefully cut in at 90°. Move the tool straight in to slice and clean up the shoulders, cutting in just deep enough to form a round. Now clean up the round ring to about 1¼ in. dia. Just under that, cut

in another ⅛ in. to reduce the diameter. Mark down 5 in. and cut a thin line at the maximum diameter (1¼ in.). Then use the diamond-point tool to cut to the bottom. To form the swell taper, I use a gouge and turn from below the transition ring to the max point, then taper gently to the bottom. Finish with sandpaper and 0000 steel wool. Add a light bevel at the bottom. On all the legs (tapered and turned), I break square corners with P220-grit sandpaper.

Define the transition point. With a very sharp diamond-point scraper held on edge, carefully cut in at 90°, clearly defining the point where the square collar ends.

Create a ¼-in. ring. With the diamond-point scraper, establish the bottom of the ring and cut in another ⅛ in. to bring the diameter down more.

Establish the maximum diameter. A mortising chisel on its edge cuts a thin line where the turned leg is at its widest point.

Form the swell. With a ½-in. gouge, start from below the transition ring and turn a gentle curve up to the thin line and then taper down gently to the bottom of the leg.

TURNED LEG

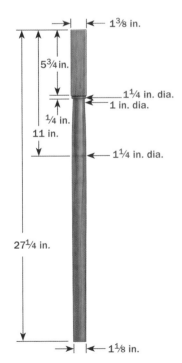

1⅜ in.

5¾ in.

1¼ in. dia.
1 in. dia.

¼ in.

11 in.

1¼ in. dia.

27¼ in.

1⅛ in.

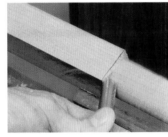

Square to round. Using a ½-in. gouge, start to turn the blank round from the line down. Turn it to its widest diameter (1¼ in.).

Fast mortises. The basic mortise-and-tenon construction makes this an easy project to tackle. A drill press and chisel are all that's needed to create the mortises. To start, mark the mortise locations on the leg, then use a fence clamped to the table to align a brad-point bit as you clear most of the mortise.

joinery, a dovetailed top rail, and a dovetailed drawer. I start with the legs, move on to the joinery, add the drawer, and finish.

Tackle the joinery: mortises, tenons, and a dovetail

Once the legs are finished (see "Two Options for Legs" on pp. 34–35), the construction is the same for both tables. The first step is to add the side and back aprons and drawer rails to the legs. I start with the mortises for the back and side aprons and the rail below the drawer. Then I cut the tenons on all of those pieces. The rail above the drawer is dovetailed into the top of the leg, and I tackle that after the mortises and tenons.

Mortise the legs

I have a dedicated slot-mortiser for this job, but a drill press and mortising chisel also will work. After you lay out the locations for the mortises, waste away the majority of the material on the drill press with a brad-point

Clean up the mortises with chisels. Mark the depth of the mortise on a mortising chisel. Starting at the ends of the mortise, tap the mortising chisel squarely in place (left). Finish by cleaning up the mortise walls with a regular bench chisel (above).

bit. Then you can use chisels to clean up the edges and ends.

Tenon the aprons and lower front stretcher

I cut the apron tenons on the tablesaw using a dado blade. There are three different blade-height settings, one for each cheek and one for the top and bottom edges. By the way, the first cheek-cut height isn't critical; it's the second one that sets the final thickness and fit of the tenons. Also, on legs this small, I try to maximize the length of the tenons, so I do end up mitering them.

I cut the lower front-rail tenons the same way as I cut the apron tenons. Then I use the shoulder-to-shoulder measurement of that piece to mark out the dovetail shoulders for the upper rail.

Dovetail the upper front rail to the legs

Once I have dry-fitted the three aprons and the bottom rail, I lay out the dovetails on both ends of the top rail, cut them with a handsaw, and refine them with a chisel. On the tablesaw, I skim a small rabbet on the underside of the dovetail, which creates a shoulder and helps locate the dovetail on the leg. Once that's done, transfer the dovetails to the tops of the front legs, using a knife. A small router with a ⅛-in. or ¼-in. bit takes out most of the waste material. Use a chisel to clean the corners.

Glue up the bases and add runners, kickers, and spacers

Before adding the runners and kickers, sand the legs, aprons, and rails to P320-grit sandpaper and glue the bases together. Begin by gluing the front legs to the rails and the back legs to the back apron in two separate assemblies. Once they are dry, add the two

Dovetailed rail adds strength. A quick dovetail locks the top rail in place and adds extra sturdiness to the whole base. Dovetail the rail and then cut the mating slots in the legs. To start, cut a rabbet on the underside of the dovetails. Use a tenoning jig. The shallow lip (1⁄16 in.) helps when you are marking the dovetail's position on the legs.

Transfer the layout to the legs. Dry-fit the lower rail to the legs, and position the upper rail across the top of the legs to transfer the dovetail profile (left). Use a small router to cut close to the line and a chisel to finish the job (right).

Fit the upper rail. A final dry-fit of the rails to the front legs ensures an accurate fit and a stress-free glue-up. These parts will be the first step of the gluing process.

side aprons as a final assembly. And once that is dry, you can glue in the runners and kickers.

The drawer runners and kickers (a pair on each side of the drawer) are the same size and shape, simply a strip of wood notched to fit between the front and back legs. The runners sit below the drawer sides and provide the track that the drawer runs on while it moves in and out of the side table. A kicker is a strip of wood that is placed above each drawer side to keep the drawer from tipping down as it is opened and closed. In addition, I use the kicker to screw the top in place. Also, because the sides are inset from the legs, I glue in a spacer just above the runner. This spacer keeps the drawer from tilting left or right.

There is no joinery involved in adding the runners and kickers; they are simply cut to fit the interior, then glued and clamped in place, flush with the top and bottom of the aprons and rails. Trim the spacers perfectly flush with the inside faces of the legs.

Hand-cut dovetails in the drawers

The drawer fronts are cut to fit the openings. I make my fronts ¾ in. thick, the back ⅝ in. thick, and the sides ½ in. thick. I make the back a little thicker than the sides for three reasons: First, thinner sides make the drawer appear more graceful, and you'll seldom pull it all the way out to see the thickness of the back. Second, the added thickness gives a bit more glue surface to the dovetails, resulting in stronger joints on all four corners. Finally, it allows a solid bottom (not plywood) to expand and contract while remaining hidden under the back.

I cut half-blind dovetails in the front and through-dovetails in the back, cutting the tails first. I make the drawer bottoms from resawn, book-matched stock and secure them with a screw and slot in the back to allow for seasonal movement.

I turn the mushroom-shaped knobs on the lathe.

Assemble in stages. Start with the front and back, gluing the back apron to the back legs and the front stretchers to the front legs. After the front and back of the base are dry, add the side aprons. Next you'll add the internal pieces that form the drawer pocket.

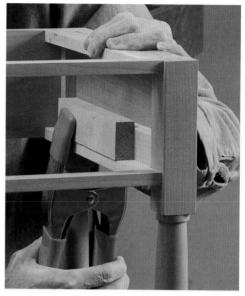

No joinery for runners, kickers, and spacers. The runners and kickers are simply glued and clamped into place, flush with the top and bottom of the aprons and rails (left). Plane the spacers perfectly flush with the inside faces of the legs before gluing them on (above).

Dovetailed drawer adds function, beauty. Here's a transfer trick: The author runs the groove for the drawer bottom on the tablesaw and then uses the groove (and a small scrap) to align the parts when transferring the tails to the pin board.

Screw the top in place

Last, I edge-glue the ¾-in.-thick top, cut it to size, sand it, and use the tablesaw to add a slight bevel to the underside. With the top facedown, I center the base (1½ in. front and back, 4 in. on the sides) and drill three countersunk holes through each of the drawer kickers (one in the center, one at either end) to screw the base to the top. I made the end holes oval-shaped to allow for wood movement.

I give the tables three coats of an oil finish. The first coat is straight Danish oil and the next two coats are a ratio of two parts Tried & True varnish oil and one part spar varnish. I use only wax on the drawer runners, spacers, kickers, and drawer sides and bottom, to help them run more smoothly.

Keep it level. Secure the pin board in a vise and use a spacer block to keep the tail board level on the pin board for layout.

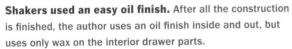

Shakers used an easy oil finish. After all the construction is finished, the author uses an oil finish inside and out, but uses only wax on the interior drawer parts.

Solid drawer bottom made easy. Cut the bottom of the drawer back to line up with the drawer groove, so the bottom can slide into place. A single screw secures the solid bottom to the back, with a slot to allow for seasonal movement.

Porringer-Top Tea Table

DAN FAIA

When a client asked for a tea table recently, I built this one in the Queen Anne porringer style, named for the top's rounded, soup bowl–shaped corners. I found the design in an antiques catalog. The original was built in Wethersfield, Conn., sometime between 1740 and 1760.

Tea tables were most popular from the William and Mary period in the early 1700s through the Empire period in the mid-1800s. Today, even though earlier dinner times have put an end to daily afternoon teas, these tables still are useful as end tables or occasional tables.

This piece is also a great way to get started in building period reproductions. The design is simple, but there are challenging details in matching the grain, shaping the cabriole legs and transition blocks, and creating the uniquely shaped top. The project requires careful machine work and a delicate touch with hand tools. When you're done, you'll have a handsome, highly functional piece of furniture.

Seek consistent grain for a coherent look

Lumber selection and grain orientation are critical details for any furniture project. Using the right grain for individual parts can make the difference between a good piece and a great one. For grain consistency, I made the aprons and the slip-matched top from a single board. It might seem shameful to rip wide lumber into narrow pieces, but it pays off in the finished appearance.

Grain selection for the cabriole legs is even more important. Look for a 12/4 board with a rift-sawn end section, but be prepared to spend some time picking through the lumber to find it. Most pieces that will fill the bill will be rift for only half or three-quarters of the width. You'll rarely find a board that will yield any more than two legs side by side in the rift.

Turn the feet before shaping the legs

Start by rough-cutting the leg blanks longer than the finished leg. This leaves matching stock for two transition blocks, which you should trim off after the leg is turned and before it is shaped.

Begin by turning the pad foot on the center of the blank. Layout is done using plywood patterns derived from full-scale drawings. On the lathe, use a parting tool and a pair of calipers to set the pad's maximum diameter and to cut the fillet on which the foot will rest. Then make a rolling cut with a spindle gouge to establish the curve between the foot's widest point and the fillet. The last step on the lathe is to use the corner of the skew to make a shallow scribing cut that just begins the top of the foot. This will help you locate the toe later in the leg-shaping process.

Rough-cut the profile on the bandsaw. After turning the pad foot, trace the layout onto two faces of the blank and cut one face (top right). Leave the waste area above the knee intact for now. Then tape the cutoffs back in place and cut the second face (bottom right). The cutoffs support the work for safe and accurate cutting of the adjacent sides.

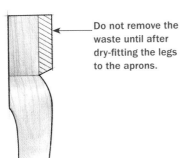

Do not remove the waste until after dry-fitting the legs to the aprons.

Two Ways to Orient the Grain

There are two options for the look of the legs: flow lines and bull's-eyes. Flow lines, used on this piece, keep a parallel vertical pattern that follows the leg's contours. Bull's-eyes are the sunburst patterns seen at the peak of the knee. You can get either pattern from the same blank, depending on how you orient the leg. End grain that runs from inside corner to outside corner will create flow lines (right). Side-to-side grain will produce bull's-eyes (far right).

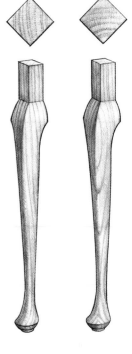

Basic Joinery
Supports a Graceful Design

Simple mortise-and-tenon joinery brings the leg posts and aprons together, while the details lend distinction to the piece. The aprons are flush with the leg posts, and the curves in the cabriole legs are echoed by the rounded corners and edge details of the tabletop.

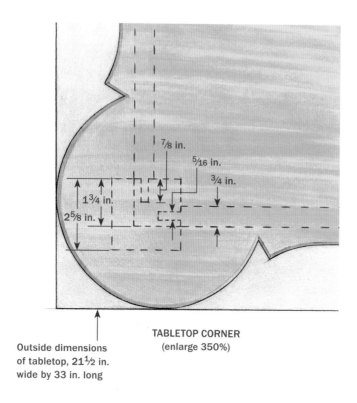

7/8 in.

5/16 in.

3/4 in.

1 3/4 in.

2 5/8 in.

Outside dimensions of tabletop, 21 1/2 in. wide by 33 in. long

TABLETOP CORNER
(enlarge 350%)

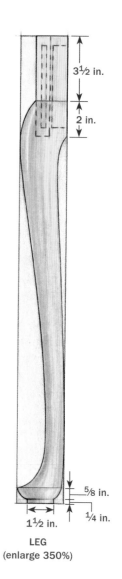

3 1/2 in.

2 in.

5/8 in.

1/4 in.

1 1/2 in.

LEG
(enlarge 350%)

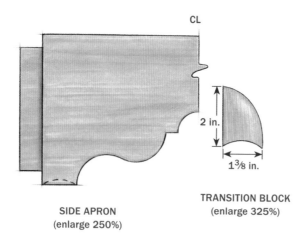

CL

2 in.

1 3/8 in.

SIDE APRON
(enlarge 250%)

TRANSITION BLOCK
(enlarge 325%)

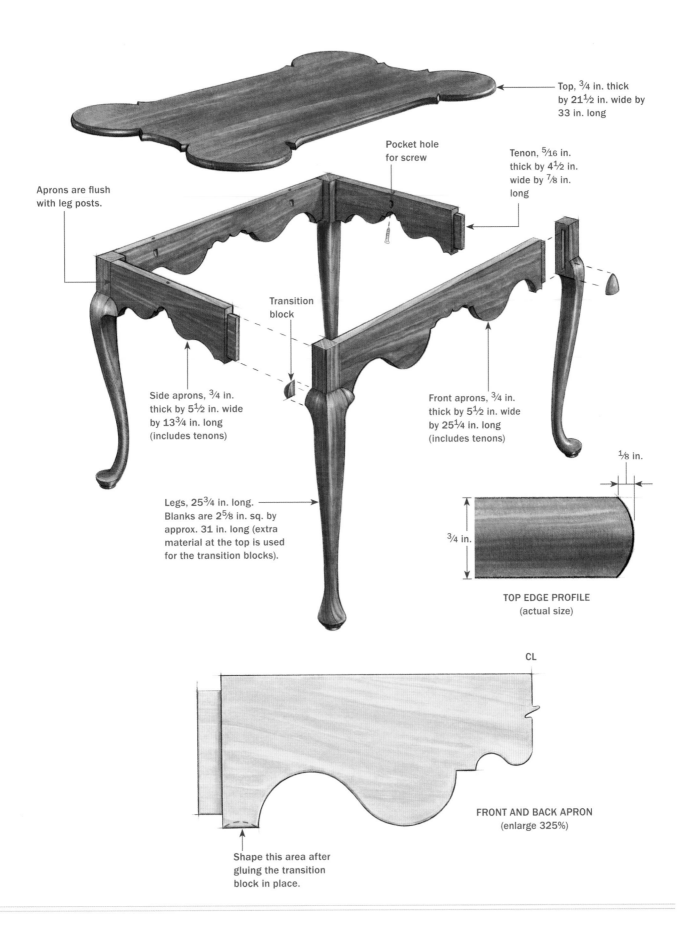

Top, ¾ in. thick
by 21½ in. wide by
33 in. long

Pocket hole
for screw

Tenon, ⁵⁄₁₆ in.
thick by 4½ in.
wide by ⅞ in.
long

Aprons are flush
with leg posts.

Transition
block

Side aprons, ¾ in.
thick by 5½ in. wide
by 13¾ in. long
(includes tenons)

Front aprons, ¾ in.
thick by 5½ in. wide
by 25¼ in. long
(includes tenons)

⅛ in.

Legs, 25¾ in. long.
Blanks are 2⅝ in. sq. by
approx. 31 in. long (extra
material at the top is used
for the transition blocks).

¾ in.

TOP EDGE PROFILE
(actual size)

CL

FRONT AND BACK APRON
(enlarge 325%)

Shape this area after
gluing the transition
block in place.

Lay Out the Primary Chamfers

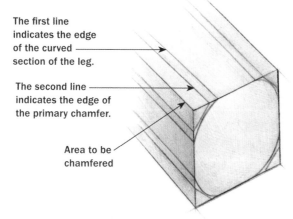

The first line indicates the edge of the curved section of the leg.

The second line indicates the edge of the primary chamfer.

Area to be chamfered

Mark the edges of the curves. Begin the layout for shaping the leg by drawing a pair of reference lines on each side, at equal distances from the corners. These are called centerlines because the two meet at the center of the leg's narrowest point.

Mark the edge of the first chamfer. The author visualizes a 5/7 ratio to draw a new set of lines a little less than halfway from the reference lines to the corner on each side. He chisels to these lines when creating the first chamfers.

While the blanks are square, cut or chop the mortises for the aprons, making sure to choose the proper inside corner for the grain selection. Label and trim off the transition blocks, and cut the legs to length.

Time-honored cabriole layout method

Lay out the leg pattern on the two inside faces and bandsaw the profile. Do not bandsaw the top of the post and stay proud of the pattern line by 1/16 in. or more above the knee. It is important to leave plenty of wood here for shaping later. Clean up the cuts with a spokeshave and a rasp, making each surface a fair curve.

I shaped the legs primarily with wide, flat chisels, removing wood in a series of chamfers until I arrived at a rounded profile. For consistency, I laid out the chamfers using a technique called the 5/7 rule.

At this small scale, the 5/7 rule isn't a precise measuring technique. It's a way of eyeballing the layout with consistent results (consistent enough, anyway, to please the eye). Start at the ankle by marking the center point of each side of the leg. From these marks, draw centerlines up and down the blank, maintaining the same dimension and following the curves created by the saw.

Your next marks should be a little less than halfway from these centerlines to each adjacent corner. To estimate this distance consistently, imagine that the space between each center point and each adjacent corner is divided into 12 equal parts. From each center, count five units toward the corners and make your marks at those locations. Draw additional layout lines from these marks up and down the blank.

Use a chisel and rasp to remove the material between these second layout lines, creating a broad chamfer. Now mark the centerlines of the chamfers. Refine the profile by paring about halfway in from these centerlines and

the original ones to remove the newly created corners. This will create a set of narrower, secondary chamfers. Last, remove the ridges along these faces with a spokeshave. The corners should now be so close to round that no other division is needed. Use a rasp, file, and scraper to achieve the final shape.

Blocks transition from apron to knee

Cut the apron stock to the appropriate lengths and rip the aprons slightly wider than the finished width. I used a dado head on the tablesaw to cut the tenons. Remove milling marks from the aprons with a handplane. Locate the center of each apron, measuring from the shoulders. Trace the apron patterns and bandsaw to shape. Clean up the bandsaw marks with a spokeshave, chisels, and files.

Cut the first chamfer. Use a chisel to remove the wood between the second layout lines (top). Stop the cut at the narrowest part of the leg, where the grain direction changes, and then work from the opposite direction. The sharply curved area just above the foot is hard to negotiate with the chisel. Follow up with a rasp to smooth the transition (above).

Lay Out the Secondary Chamfers

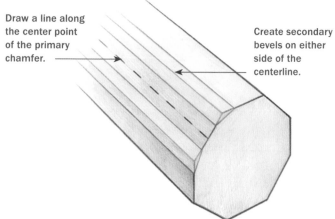

Draw a line along the center point of the primary chamfer. →

Create secondary bevels on either side of the centerline.

Lay out the next chamfers. Mark centerlines on the newly created faces. These lines will be used in cutting a second set of chamfers.

Cut the new facets. Chisel away a triangular section of waste between the two centerlines. This cut is only about halfway to the line on either side of the corner (above). The remaining ridges are small enough to remove with a spokeshave (top right). Use rasps, files, and sandpaper to shape the leg to its finished contour (bottom right).

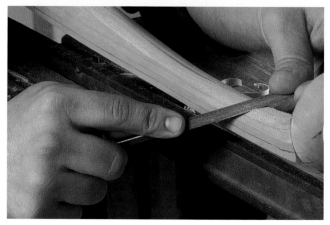

Profile the aprons. Use chisels, rasps, and files to create a smooth surface after bandsawing the apron shape.

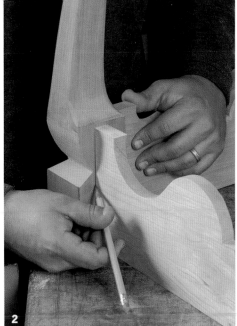

Mark and trim the posts. Dry-fit the aprons into the mortised leg posts and trace cut lines on the front of each post (2). The finished posts will be flush with the aprons. Cut on the waste side of the line and plane the posts flush with the apron after glue-up (3).

With the base dry-fitted together, trace the outside face of the aprons onto the leg posts, which were left fat earlier. Bandsaw the posts just proud of these lines, leaving wood that can be planed flush to the aprons after assembly. Glue up the base, checking for square and using moderate clamp pressure. Finish the assembly by trimming the posts flush to the apron fronts with a shoulder plane.

To begin fitting the transition blocks, first handplane their mating surfaces so they fit tightly to the legs and aprons. Now clamp the transition block temporarily into place, aligning it roughly with the flat bottom of the apron and use it as a reference surface for the shoulder plane. You want to plane the top of the leg where it meets the post, bringing its height flush with the top of the transition block.

Glue up the base. Use moderate clamping pressure and be sure to check the assembly for square.

Prep the leg for corner blocks. Plane the post flush. Use a shoulder plane, referencing off the surface of the apron.

Locate the transition block. Clamp the rough stock in place, aligned roughly with the bottom of the apron. Plane the top of the leg to match the block's height.

Add transition blocks. Mark and cut the corner block. Mark the block at the knee's apex to determine its thickness (above). Cut the block to shape and glue it in place before shaping it with a chisel (right).

Remove the blocks and use a bandsaw to cut the curved side profiles on each one. Use chisels and sandpaper to smooth the outer profiles to a fair shape, and then glue the blocks onto the legs and aprons. Chisel the leg profile to shape with the transition blocks. Curve the transitions across their width from the leg to the apron. Continue shaping diagonally over the blocks to a final rounding.

Shape and attach the top

I like to spring-joint the top boards. To *spring* the joint, plane away a minimal amount of wood from the middle section of each edge, so clamping pressure is moderate.

Then the joint requires only one center clamp for glue-up. After planing and/or sanding the top flat, lay out and bandsaw the top pattern slightly proud of the lines. A jigsaw is a good alternative for cutting these shapes, especially the large-radius corners. Fairing these shapes by hand will require the use of many tools—spokeshave, chisel, file, and scraper.

The edge profile is not a half-round shape. It's a section of a larger radius, which is a common profile used in 18th-century furniture. Layout is simple. Draw a single centerline on the edge and a pair of lines (one on each face) marking the top and bottom of the curve.

Shape the transition block. Pare across the top of the block, using the leg as a reference surface. As you near the apron, round over the ledge made by the shoulder plane.

Change directions. Next, work toward the top of the leg, rounding the transition block until it meets the apron.

The makers of many original pieces used glue blocks to attach their tabletops; however, I don't recommend this because it restricts seasonal movement. Six wood screws, driven through pocket holes in the aprons, hold this top down. Mount the two end screws tightly and widen the slots for the four side screws to allow for wood movement.

Fair the curves underneath. Use a rasp to smooth the underside of the transition block where it meets the bottom of the apron.

Shaping the tabletop's edge. Using chisels, rasps, and files, work between a centerline drawn on the edge and the layout lines on the faces.

Arts and Crafts Side Table

KELLY J. DUNTON

The inspiration for this table dates back a century to designs by Gustav Stickley. He defined his furniture philosophy as being "where the beauty lies in simplicity of the wood and of the joints themselves." To be faithful to the original designs, I built my table from white oak with pegged through-tenons joining the lower stretchers to the legs.

There are many uses for a small table: With slight changes in size, it can sit next to a chair in the family room, serve as a bedside table, or be used as a plant stand. Made from cherry or maple, this design would fit nicely into more modern decor.

This is a relatively simple project that uses little material and can be built with common hand tools and machines. So sharpen your chisels and planes and let's get started.

Lay out the legs and cut the mortises

Much but not all furniture in this style was made from quartersawn white oak with its characteristic ray flecks running across the grain on opposite sides of the board. I chose this type of wood for the prominent top of the table, but for the rest of the piece I used more readily available rift-sawn boards (see "Lower Stretcher Detail" on p. 54).

Because three sides of each leg will have near equal exposure to the viewer, I cut and surfaced the legs to size, and then selected the least attractive side of each leg to face inward. When laying out the mortises, make sure to place them accurately on all the legs and make sure the leg dimensions are identical; this will keep the table square and stable. Because the lower stretchers end in through-tenons instead of the more common blind tenons, remember to mark both sides of the legs using the same side as a reference edge. I lay out the mortises using a marking gauge, a square, and a knife. I prefer a knife to a pencil because it gives greater precision and allows you to set the chisel in the knife cut later for the final paring cuts. These joints will be exposed, so take the time to lay out and cut them precisely.

There are several ways to cut the mortises. A hollow-chisel mortiser is the quickest method, but lacking this tool I chose to remove most of the waste at the drill press and then clean up the sides and ends with a sharp chisel. (Drilling by hand is an option, but it is important to drill straight and true.) To hold the workpiece securely and to prevent tearout on the bottom side of each leg, make a small fence consisting of two pieces of plywood or medium-density fiberboard (MDF) glued and screwed at a 90° angle, which gets clamped to the drill-press table.

Install a bit that is slightly smaller than the width of the mortise, center the mortise on the bit, and then drill out the waste, starting at each end. It's best to use a Forstner bit because you can overlap the holes without causing the bit to wander off course. A

Side Table

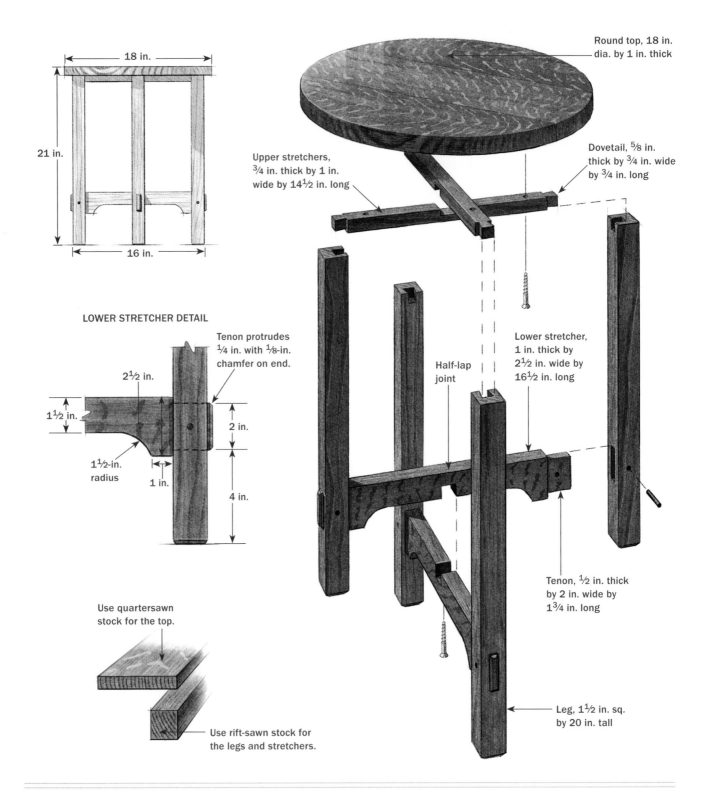

18 in.

21 in.

16 in.

Round top, 18 in.
dia. by 1 in. thick

Upper stretchers,
$\frac{3}{4}$ in. thick by 1 in.
wide by 14$\frac{1}{2}$ in. long

Dovetail, $\frac{5}{8}$ in.
thick by $\frac{3}{4}$ in. wide
by $\frac{3}{4}$ in. long

LOWER STRETCHER DETAIL

Tenon protrudes
$\frac{1}{4}$ in. with $\frac{1}{8}$-in.
chamfer on end.

2$\frac{1}{2}$ in.

1$\frac{1}{2}$ in.

2 in.

1$\frac{1}{2}$-in.
radius

1 in.

4 in.

Half-lap
joint

Lower stretcher,
1 in. thick by
2$\frac{1}{2}$ in. wide by
16$\frac{1}{2}$ in. long

Use quartersawn
stock for the top.

Use rift-sawn stock for
the legs and stretchers.

Tenon, $\frac{1}{2}$ in. thick
by 2 in. wide by
1$\frac{3}{4}$ in. long

Leg, 1$\frac{1}{2}$ in. sq.
by 20 in. tall

second choice is a brad-point bit—cut the holes as close to each other as possible without overlapping.

With the leg clamped to the workbench, clean up each end of the mortise using a chisel that matches the mortise width as closely as possible. Keep the chisel off the layout line until the final cut, which should remove only a sliver of wood. Work into the center from both sides, but try to get the cleanest cuts on the visible outside of the leg. With the mortise ends established, use the widest chisel that will fit the length of the mortise to pare the sides. Working with white oak will probably require a mallet and a few trips to your sharpening stones. With patience and determination, you'll soon have clean mortises.

Create the upper and lower stretchers

With the legs nearly complete, turn to the upper and lower stretchers. Both pairs are connected with half-lap joints, but the lower stretchers have a curved profile on the bottom edges and terminate in through-tenons. I used a marking gauge, a try square, and a marking knife to lay out the tenons.

Drill the mortises. To keep the mortises straight and square and to prevent tearout where the bit exits, a jig consisting of a backer board and a right-angle fence is clamped to the drill-press table (above). With a Forstner bit, you can overlap each hole and remove more waste (right).

Clean up the mortises. Use a chisel the same width as the mortises to clean up the ends (left) and then a wider chisel on the sides (right). Creep up to the line. Don't place the tip of the chisel in the line left by the marking knife until you have only a thin slice of wood to remove.

Tenons on the tablesaw. Use a dado set for quick tenons. For accuracy and clean cuts, outfit the miter gauge with an auxiliary fence and a stop block. Through-tenons must look good and fit right, so clean them up with a shoulder plane, a block plane, and/or a chisel.

Cut the half laps. With the same miter gauge and auxiliary fence used to cut the tenons, cut the half-lap joint on each stretcher.

Profile the stretchers. Join the lower stretchers with double-faced tape and then bandsaw the profile.

Chamfer the tenons and legs. A ⅛-in. bevel gives the exposed through-tenons and leg bottoms a softer look and creates interesting shadow lines.

I cut the tenons using a dado blade on the tablesaw. It is helpful to make test cuts on a piece of scrap the same thickness as the stretchers. Check the fit until it is still a bit fat, and then pare the tenons with a block plane, a shoulder plane, or a chisel. In this way, you will get a precise fit and nice clean cuts on the exposed tenon ends. Number each joint when you are done.

Now mark and cut the half-lap joints in both pairs of stretchers. Work from the center points of each pair and mark the widths of each at the crossing point. Mark for the depth from the top of each stretcher and label which side is to be removed. Using a miter gauge, make multiple passes on the tablesaw to remove most of the waste. Then pare with a chisel to a perfect fit.

To bandsaw the profile on both lower stretchers at once, join them with double-faced tape. The curve also can be cut with a jigsaw, but clamp or tape a piece of scrap to the upper side of the stretcher to keep the cut as clean as possible.

When the upper stretchers are cut to size, saw a dovetail on each end. A handsaw and/or tablesaw can make these cuts, leaving just a bit of chisel work. Cut a ⅛-in. shoulder on the lower side. This shoulder can be registered against the side of the leg to transfer the shape of the dovetail to the top of the leg. After laying out the mortises in the legs, remove some of the waste on the drill press and then clamp the leg in a vise and chop away the rest with a chisel.

The final work on the top stretchers is to drill and countersink screw holes through which to attach the tabletop. To allow for seasonal movement of the top, elongate the holes in one of the stretchers.

Dovetail the upper stretchers. Saw a dovetail onto the ends of the upper stretchers. Dry-fit the table and scribe the location of the dovetail on the top of each leg (1). Saw on the scribe mark (2) and remove most of the waste on the drill press. Clean up the joint with a chisel (3).

Make the round tabletop

It is worth spending time at the wood supplier searching for a quartersawn board with a decent amount of ray fleck in it to form the tabletop. Making the top from three well-matched pieces from a single board is better than using two wider but conflicting pieces from different boards. Prepare, glue up, and clamp the pieces.

There are many ways to cut the circular top. The simplest is freehand, using either a bandsaw or a jigsaw and cleaning up the edge with hand tools and sandpaper. I used the bandsaw, but with a jig that sits in the miter-gauge slot and has a center point that fits into the underside of the tabletop (see "Build a Simple Circle Jig" below). Slide the jig until the front edge of the blade is aligned with the center of the tabletop, and rotate the top until the circle is complete. Clean up the edge with a block plane, file, and sandpaper.

Build a Simple Circle Jig

To cut the circular top, the author uses a jig that sits in the miter-gauge slot and has a dowel that fits into a hole drilled in the underside of the tabletop. The distance from the side of the jig that touches the bandsaw blade to the dowel equals the tabletop radius. Slide the jig until the front edge of the blade is aligned with the center of the dowel, and insert the stop screw.

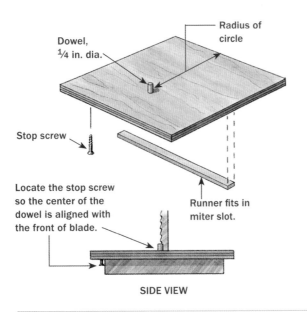

Dowel, ¼ in. dia.

Radius of circle

Stop screw

Locate the stop screw so the center of the dowel is aligned with the front of blade.

Runner fits in miter slot.

SIDE VIEW

Use the circle jig. Place the tabletop on the jig and slide it forward until the stop screw hits the saw table (top). Then rotate the top to cut the circle (above).

Assemble the base in two stages. To begin base assembly, glue and clamp the first pair of legs to their upper and lower stretchers. On the second pair of legs, glue only the lower stretcher in place.

Assembly sequence and finishing

To be historically accurate I decided on a fumed finish, which uses ammonia fumes to darken the oak chemically and is best done with the piece dry-fitted. As for a topcoat, whether you fume the oak or prefer a natural look, it is beneficial to prefinish the pieces before assembling them.

Sand all surfaces to P220-grit and then carefully wipe a clear finish on all the surfaces that will not be glued, including the ends of each tenon, which will protrude from the legs.

Begin assembly by preparing the mortises for pinning. I marked the center points of the mortise sides and drilled all the way through using a sharp brad-point bit with a piece of scrap under the leg to minimize breakout. After the stretchers are glued to the legs, you'll drill into the existing hole and through the tenon before inserting ebony pins.

Glue the first pair of legs and stretchers and clamp until dry. Apply glue just to the tenons

Finish the base assembly. Because you need to overlap the two halves of the base, attach the second upper stretcher only after the lower stretchers are together.

Peg the joints. The pegs are inserted from both sides of the leg to avoid blowing out the wood when they exit.

after they have been partially inserted into the mortises to reduce squeeze-out. The second pair overlaps the first, so don't glue in the second top stretcher until after the two pairs of legs are connected. I drove a screw into the bottom of the lower intersecting stretchers.

Shaker-Inspired Hall Table

CHRISTIAN BECKSVOORT

This long, narrow table, which I designed years ago, is a kind of chameleon. You can use it in a variety of ways and in all sorts of places: as a hall table, a display table, behind a couch, or even as a sideboard-like serving table. No matter where you put this piece, it looks good. The design is sturdy but looks light and attractive, thanks in large part to the splay of the turned and tapered legs.

Unless I'm doing an exact Shaker reproduction, I splay all table legs that are turned and tapered. Otherwise, they tend to look pigeon-toed and slightly unstable. And for a long, narrow table like this, there's more than just appearance at stake. The splayed legs make the base wider at the floor than under the top, giving it a surer stance.

Light and Lively

The author varies his table from straight Shaker by splaying the legs. Arched aprons add to the sense of lightness.

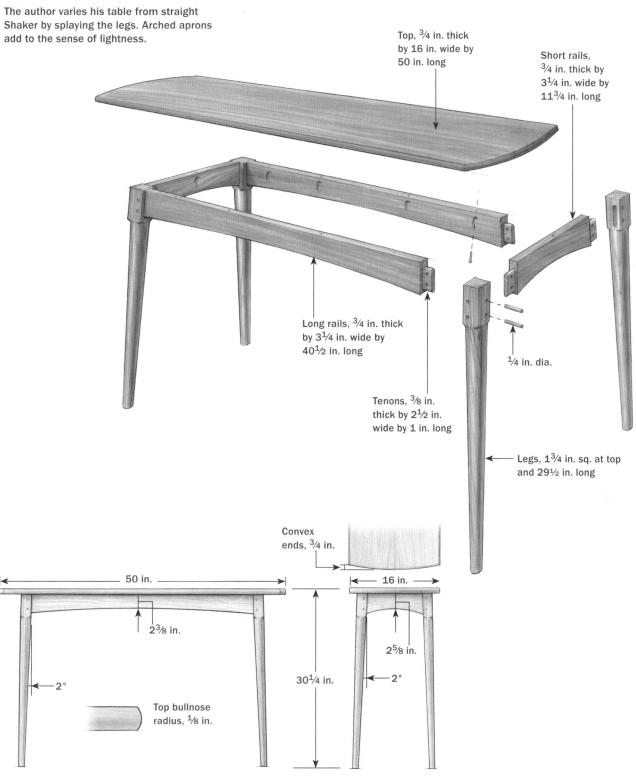

Top, 3/4 in. thick by 16 in. wide by 50 in. long

Short rails, 3/4 in. thick by 3 1/4 in. wide by 11 3/4 in. long

Long rails, 3/4 in. thick by 3 1/4 in. wide by 40 1/2 in. long

Tenons, 3/8 in. thick by 2 1/2 in. wide by 1 in. long

1/4 in. dia.

Legs, 1 3/4 in. sq. at top and 29 1/2 in. long

Convex ends, 3/4 in.

50 in.

2 3/8 in.

2°

Top bullnose radius, 1/8 in.

16 in.

2 5/8 in.

2°

30 1/4 in.

Taper the Leg

You don't need to be a full-time turner to make perfect tapers. The author marks the high spots with one long block and sands them smooth and straight with another.

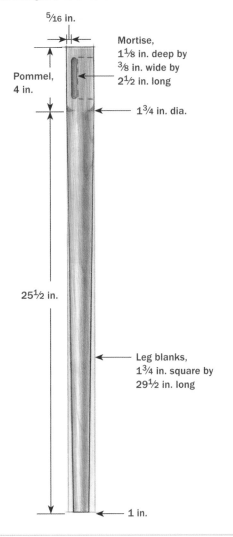

5⁄16 in.

Mortise,
1⅛ in. deep by
⅜ in. wide by
2½ in. long

Pommel,
4 in.

1¾ in. dia.

25½ in.

Leg blanks,
1¾ in. square by
29½ in. long

1 in.

For the maker, part of the beauty is that this gently splayed stance is easy to create with just a few simple, angled cuts at the tablesaw. This project is perfect for getting acquainted with angled joinery and for working with the lathe. The angles are all small and easy to cut, and the turning won't overwhelm you. I'll show you a no-nonsense way to get a nice straight taper on those legs, a deceptively difficult turning task.

A straight approach to round legs

These legs are square at the top where they join the aprons, with the turned portion beginning 4 in. from the top. The most difficult part of the turning is cleanly cutting this transition from square to round.

With the blank centered in the lathe and the transition point marked on the stock, set the lathe at approximately 2,200 rpm and use a ½-in. spindle gouge to turn away from the

From square to round. After turning the first few inches of the round section with a spindle gouge, use a diamond-point tool (inset) to cut a clean bevel at the transition (1). Lay out the beginning of the cut and then plunge in at 45°. A 45° mark on the tool rest is a good visual guide. Afterward, use a roughing gouge to rough in the taper (2).

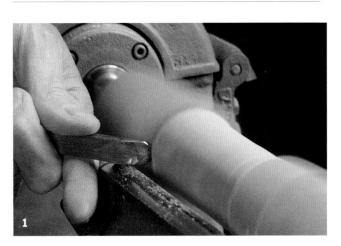

Mark like magic. To identify high spots on the turning, start by covering one edge of a hardwood block with pencil lead.

Pressed into action. Held against the spinning workpiece, the block leaves graphite on the high points. Use the spindle gouge to take down these areas, then repeat until the taper is as straight as possible.

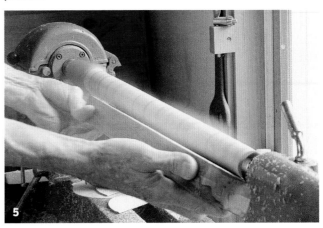

Super sanding block. Use a straight piece of stock, one face covered with 80- to 100-grit sandpaper, to straighten the taper. Then hand-sand through 400-grit and burnish with 0000 steel wool.

mark until you have a few inches of true round. Next cut the transition using a diamond-point tool held on edge, carefully entering the cut at about a 45° angle. It takes a steady hand to make this cut without knocking off the square corners; I suggest practicing on cheap stock until you master the technique.

Once this is done, use a roughing gouge to start cutting the taper at the bottom of the leg, checking your progress with a pair of calipers until you've reached the 1-in. bottom diameter. Then use the gouge to connect the top and bottom diameters. I'm a furniture maker, not a turner, so I don't bother trying to get a perfect taper and smooth finished surface with the gouge or a skew chisel. Instead, I get the results I'm looking for from a 2-ft.-long piece of hardwood. I color one edge with pencil graphite and hold it against the turning while it's spinning. The graphite marks the high points, which I then take down with a gouge or skew chisel. After three or four tries, the taper should be fairly straight, but not perfect.

The other side of the hardwood piece (or use a separate piece, if you prefer) is covered with 80- or 100-grit sandpaper. Holding that edge against the spinning taper ensures flatness. I then hand-sand the spinning leg with

Sanding Block

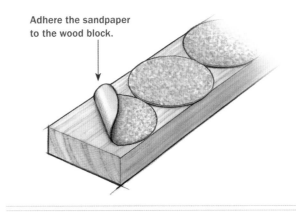

Adhere the sandpaper to the wood block.

Angle the Shoulders to Create the Splay

Each apron and leg assembly is splayed as a unit, so the joinery is angled but simple: one angle per joint.

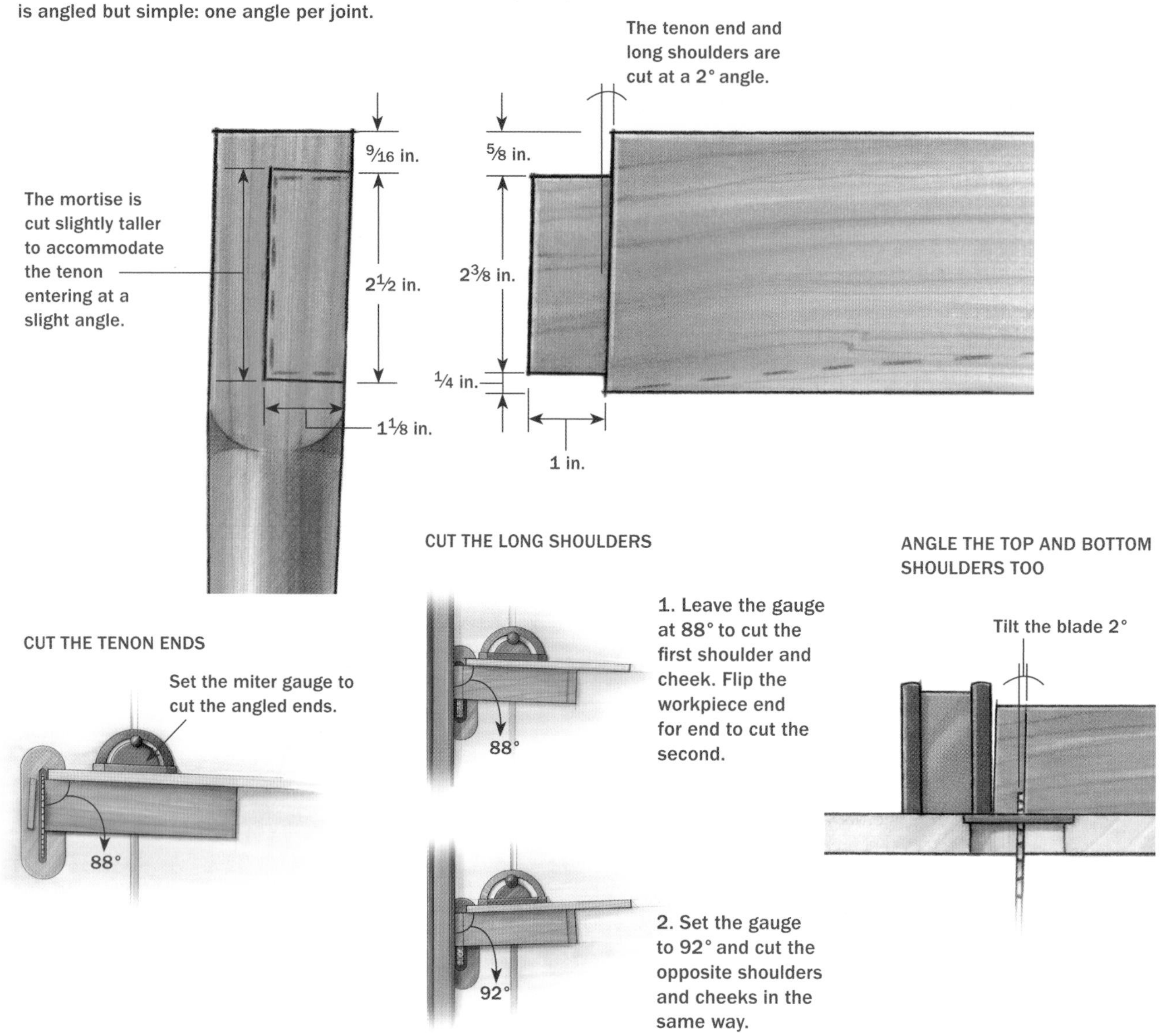

The tenon end and long shoulders are cut at a 2° angle.

The mortise is cut slightly taller to accommodate the tenon entering at a slight angle.

9/16 in.

5/8 in.

2½ in.

2⅜ in.

¼ in.

1⅛ in.

1 in.

CUT THE TENON ENDS

Set the miter gauge to cut the angled ends.

88°

CUT THE LONG SHOULDERS

1. Leave the gauge at 88° to cut the first shoulder and cheek. Flip the workpiece end for end to cut the second.

88°

2. Set the gauge to 92° and cut the opposite shoulders and cheeks in the same way.

92°

ANGLE THE TOP AND BOTTOM SHOULDERS TOO

Tilt the blade 2°

150-, 220-, and 400-grit sandpaper, stopping the lathe between grits to sand with the grain. Last, I use 0000 steel wool for a smooth, glossy surface that is ready for a finish.

Before moving on to the aprons, go ahead and cut the mortises on two adjacent sides of the square sections of the legs. The mortises are cut at the usual 90°. Putting the splay in the table's legs is a matter of cutting some fairly simple angled joinery on the aprons. That's next.

Easy way to splay

The ends of the tenons, and the tenon shoulders, are cut at a 2° angle, making each apron longer at the bottom than it is at the top. When the resulting joints come together,

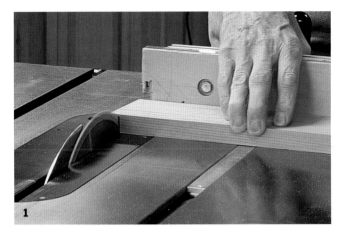

Where the splay comes from. Angle the ends of the pieces, which become the reference for angling the shoulders.

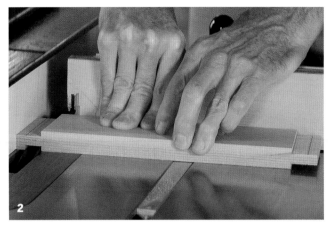

Why dado? A dado set cuts the cheeks and shoulders at the same time. Angle the miter gauge until the end of the workpiece rests flush against the fence.

Final cuts. Tilt the blade 2° to match the angle of the existing shoulder. You can cut two pieces at once. Then sever the waste at the bandsaw.

the tops of the legs lean inward and the feet splay out. You might think you need compound-angled shoulders, but because the aprons tilt with the legs, you don't.

With the apron stock milled to final thickness and width, trim each workpiece to length with a 2° angled crosscut on the tablesaw. Pay attention to the orientation of the piece for each cut—make sure that each end is angled in the right direction.

When all the ends are cut, switch to a stacked dado set, which will let you cut the tenon cheeks and shoulders simultaneously. You'll once again guide the cuts with the angled miter gauge, this time using the

tablesaw's fence to stop the cut at the tenon shoulder. *Note:* You'll be able to cut only one cheek and shoulder on each tenon with your initial miter-gauge setup. To cut the opposite sides at the correct angle, you'll need to reset the gauge to 2° in the other direction. I find it easier to make all of the cuts at one setting first, before resetting the gauge.

Last, I cut the top and bottom shoulders, standing the workpieces on edge against the miter gauge and angling the blade to make the cut. I finish the work at the bandsaw, running the workpiece against the fence to sever the waste and complete the tenons. To make sure that this straight tenon has room to fit when the mortise is angled, I plan for a little top-to-bottom slop in the fit, and I use a knife to make wedge-shaped trims as needed for clearance.

Angled cuts create a flat surface

At this point, you can dry-fit the legs and aprons, holding the assembly together with a band clamp to see how the joints fit.

With the base together, you'll see that the top edges of the aprons—and the top inside corner of each leg—all tilt inward. So the next step is to make all of these surfaces flat

Bevel the Top of the Base to Match

When the base is dry-fit, the top of each component will be canted inward. So it's necessary to trim the top edges level.

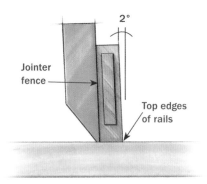

2°

Jointer
fence

Top edges
of rails

Two degrees of separation. With the highlighted corner at the bottom rear, a compound cut on the tablesaw removes a thin wedge of material.

COMPOUND CUT AT TOPS OF LEGS
Set the blade angle.

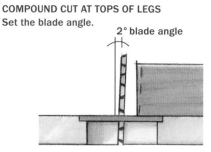

2° blade angle

Set the miter angle.

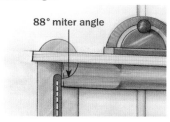

88° miter angle

Flatten the apron tops. With the jointer fence at a 2° angle, trim the apron tops so they'll be flush against the tabletop.

Same for the legs. To mark the top of the leg for trimming, start by marking the inside corner (red dot). Begin the layout at this corner. Use a bevel gauge set at a 2° angle to carry the lines around the corners.

and in the same plane to accommodate the top. To do this, disassemble the base and run the tops of the aprons over the jointer with the fence tilted 2°. Mark the pieces carefully and make sure you orient them on the jointer so that the correct portion of the top edge (the outside corner) is removed.

Trimming the tops of the legs at the proper angle requires a compound cut. The cut itself is easy to execute, but you'll need to pay attention to the layout and the setup on your tablesaw. To make it as foolproof as possible, I use a pencil or colored marker to darken the inside corner on the top of each leg. That corner should remain after the cut is made. Next, use a bevel gauge set at 2° to strike pencil lines marking the cuts on the two inside faces.

On a saw with a left-tilting blade, orient the workpiece with the marked corner riding the table at the rear of the cut. Tilt the blade 2° and angle the miter-gauge fence clockwise the same amount. Position the stock so the blade just removes the layout line on the leading edge of the workpiece.

A short length of ⅜-in. stock under the narrow end of the leg will give you greater control during the cut. You may also find it helpful to practice on a piece of 1¾-in.-square scrap first.

With these cuts made and the joinery fitted, the reassembled base should now have a flat top with all eight parts flush and in the same plane. The table's feet will not sit flat on the floor at this point, but I don't flatten them until the top is attached, in case the slightest warp or stress in the top causes the base to skew.

Arches make the piece look light

Before glue-up, cut the arches into the lower edges of the aprons. To lay out the curves, I clamp a flexible straightedge between the jaws of a bar clamp, tightening until I reach the desired amount of bow.

For visual harmony, it's important to vary the amount of bow between the long side aprons and the short ends—a shallower bow will appear more pronounced on the shorter pieces. On the long aprons, I put the top of the bow at 2⅜ in. from the top of the apron. On the ends, the apex should be 2⅝ in. from the top. Cut the arch on the bandsaw and smooth the curve with a spokeshave or sand by hand.

All four rails and the square portions of the legs should now be sanded to 400-grit, glued, and pinned. I usually glue up the two long sides first, pin them, and then glue in the short rails and pin them.

Finish up the base. Lay out the apron arches. A flexible straightedge and a bar clamp create an easily varied, regular arc for tracing. Bandsaw the curves and sand them smooth.

Drill Pocket Holes in the Aprons

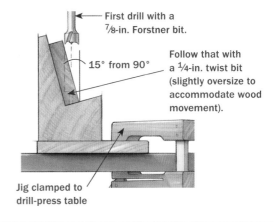

First drill with a ⅞-in. Forstner bit.

15° from 90°

Follow that with a ¼-in. twist bit (slightly oversize to accommodate wood movement).

Jig clamped to drill-press table

Pocket-hole jig for the drill press. A shop-built fence holds the inverted aprons at an angle to drill for the screws that will anchor the top to the base.

Peg the aprons to the legs. After gluing up each joint, the author drills through the leg and through the tenon for a walnut peg (above). The pin adds interest and offers a bit more joint strength. With the side assemblies glued up, join them with the end aprons (below). Use bar clamps with rubber pads on the jaws to accommodate the angled legs.

Subtle curves accent the top

The top of this table is 16 in. wide. Ideally, a single board would look the most attractive, but stock that wide is not always available. So I use an 8-in. or 9-in. board, 9 ft. to 10 ft. long, cut in half, matched as well as possible, and glued side to side. After the glue is dry, I cut the top to exact width and length.

Bandsaw a convex ¾-in. curve on the ends, again using a straightedge and clamp. All four edges are then given a slight bullnose radius with either a router or a block plane and sandpaper. Finally, smooth the top with a handplane or by sanding to at least 400-grit and polishing with 0000 steel wool.

To attach the top, center the base upside down on the underside of the top. I anchor the two end holes with drill bits (or 16d nails) and use an awl to transfer the positions of the side holes to the underside of the top. I drill slightly oversize holes along the sides to accommodate seasonal movement in the top. Now screw the base to the top.

Shape and attach the top. After cutting and smoothing a shallow arc in each end of the top, the author shapes a slight bullnose profile on all four edges, end grain first (above). To attach the top, the author centers the base, then uses a scratch awl to transfer the hole locations, predrills the tabletop, and drives the screws (right).

Flatten the feet. Plane a pencil to flatten one side slightly and use it to mark the feet for trimming with a rasp. Afterward, chamfer the circumference with a file.

Good trick for leveling legs

The last step before finishing is to flatten the bottoms of the legs. Turn the table right side up and set it on a reliably flat surface.

I position a pencil flat on this surface to trace around each leg, turn the table upside down, and use a rasp and file to trim to the lines. I rasp each foot flat then use a file to add a small chamfer all the way around.

To finish the table, I remove the top and oil the table with a 50/50 mix of Tried & True varnish oil and spar varnish. After letting it dry for 24 hours, I rub everything down with 0000 steel wool, then add two or three more coats.

After letting it dry for 24 hours, I rub everything down with 0000 steal wool, then add two or three more coats.

A Graceful Hall Table

KEVIN KAUFFUNGER

I was introduced to the work of Edward Barnsley while studying furniture making at the College of the Redwoods. Among the more dog-eared books in the school's library was an out-of-print catalog from a retrospective exhibit of his work that took place in the early 1980s. I was immediately inspired.

Barnsley was a direct descendant of the English Arts and Crafts movement (his architect father and uncle were major proponents). His early pieces were typical of the style: solid wood, thick, with exposed joinery that communicated a visual and literal strength. After World War II, his work transitioned into something more refined.

It still maintained the technical honesty of Arts and Crafts, but it began to reflect the spare elegance seen in the Hepplewhite or Federal styles.

This sideboard is not a direct copy of any Barnsley piece, but rather it incorporates many of his design elements. The construction process is relatively straightforward, so I'll focus on the Barnsley elements.

Flowing joinery

Where the legs meet the bottom rails, the lower edge of the joint flows in a continuous curve. Just joining the two members at right angles would leave weak short grain on the tip of the rail. To minimize this problem, craftsmen use a type of haunched miter called a gunstock joint, combined with slip tenons.

Lay out the legs on a template of ⅛-in.-thick plywood or MDF, transcribe the pattern onto the leg blanks, and mark out the mortises. Next, mark the 45° angle at the bisection of each curve, and with your tablesaw blade at 45°, use a crosscut sled to cut the miter ¼ in. deep into the legs, for a total of eight cuts.

Cut the mortises in your preferred way; I use an up-cutting spiral bit in a plunge router equipped with an edge guide. Mortising before shaping gives you easier surfaces to reference the router against. On the adjoining lower rails, cut matching mortises and then cut the miter using the same crosscut sled setup that you used on the legs.

Use a bandsaw to rip from the top of the leg down to the peak of the miter, reducing this portion of the leg to 1⅜ in. sq. Clean up the bandsaw marks with a block plane. You're now ready to taper and curve the leg on the bandsaw. You can use the template to guide a router bit first or do all the cleanup with hand tools, but whatever method you choose, make sure not to fully shape the curve

(continued on p. 75)

Barnsley Is in the Details

The pencil roll adds a stylish touch to the back of the tabletop and prevents objects from sliding off.

Stringing emphasizes the shapes of the tabletop and drawer fronts and leads the eye to handmade drop pulls.

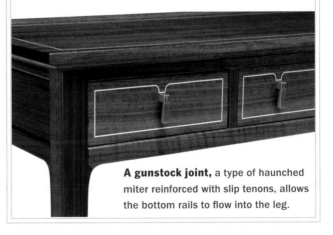

A gunstock joint, a type of haunched miter reinforced with slip tenons, allows the bottom rails to flow into the leg.

Three-Drawer Hall Table

The narrow depth makes this table suitable for halls or behind a sofa.

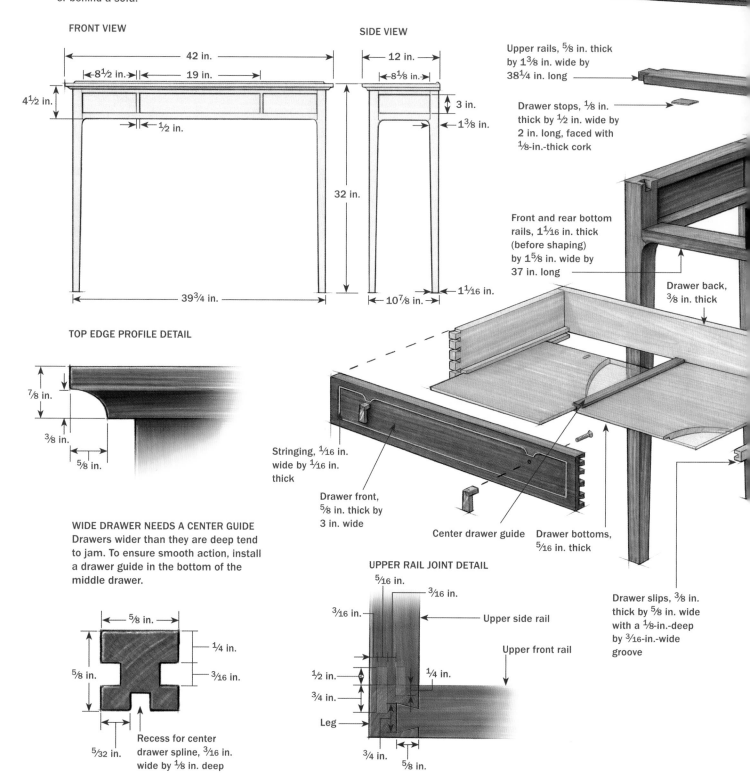

Top (less pencil roll), $7/8$ in. thick by $11^3/8$ in. wide by 42 in. long

FRONT VIEW

42 in.

$8^1/2$ in.

19 in.

$4^1/2$ in.

$1/2$ in.

$39^3/4$ in.

SIDE VIEW

12 in.

$8^1/8$ in.

3 in.

$1^3/8$ in.

32 in.

$10^7/8$ in.

$1^1/16$ in.

Upper rails, $5/8$ in. thick by $1^3/8$ in. wide by $38^1/4$ in. long

Drawer stops, $1/8$ in. thick by $1/2$ in. wide by 2 in. long, faced with $1/8$-in.-thick cork

Front and rear bottom rails, $1^1/16$ in. thick (before shaping) by $1^5/8$ in. wide by 37 in. long

Drawer back, $3/8$ in. thick

TOP EDGE PROFILE DETAIL

$7/8$ in.

$3/8$ in.

$5/8$ in.

Stringing, $1/16$ in. wide by $1/16$ in. thick

Drawer front, $5/8$ in. thick by 3 in. wide

Center drawer guide

Drawer bottoms, $5/16$ in. thick

Drawer slips, $3/8$ in. thick by $5/8$ in. wide with a $1/8$-in.-deep by $3/16$-in.-wide groove

WIDE DRAWER NEEDS A CENTER GUIDE

Drawers wider than they are deep tend to jam. To ensure smooth action, install a drawer guide in the bottom of the middle drawer.

$5/8$ in.

$5/8$ in.

$1/4$ in.

$3/16$ in.

$5/32$ in.

Recess for center drawer spline, $3/16$ in. wide by $1/8$ in. deep

UPPER RAIL JOINT DETAIL

$5/16$ in.

$3/16$ in.

$3/16$ in.

Upper side rail

Upper front rail

$1/2$ in.

$3/4$ in.

$1/4$ in.

Leg

$3/4$ in.

$5/8$ in.

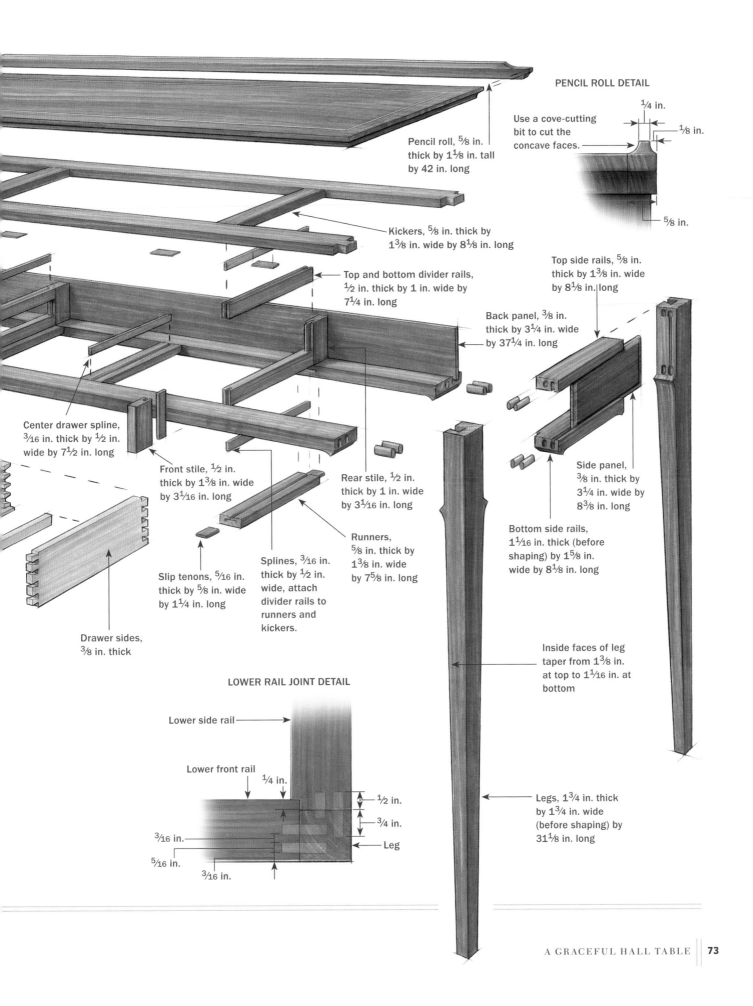

Pencil roll, $\frac{5}{8}$ in. thick by $1\frac{1}{8}$ in. tall by 42 in. long

PENCIL ROLL DETAIL

Use a cove-cutting bit to cut the concave faces.

$\frac{1}{4}$ in.

$\frac{1}{8}$ in.

$\frac{5}{8}$ in.

Kickers, $\frac{5}{8}$ in. thick by $1\frac{3}{8}$ in. wide by $8\frac{1}{8}$ in. long

Top side rails, $\frac{5}{8}$ in. thick by $1\frac{3}{8}$ in. wide by $8\frac{1}{8}$ in. long

Top and bottom divider rails, $\frac{1}{2}$ in. thick by 1 in. wide by $7\frac{1}{4}$ in. long

Back panel, $\frac{3}{8}$ in. thick by $3\frac{1}{4}$ in. wide by $37\frac{1}{4}$ in. long

Center drawer spline, $\frac{3}{16}$ in. thick by $\frac{1}{2}$ in. wide by $7\frac{1}{2}$ in. long

Side panel, $\frac{3}{8}$ in. thick by $3\frac{1}{4}$ in. wide by $8\frac{3}{8}$ in. long

Front stile, $\frac{1}{2}$ in. thick by $1\frac{3}{8}$ in. wide by $3\frac{1}{16}$ in. long

Rear stile, $\frac{1}{2}$ in. thick by 1 in. wide by $3\frac{1}{16}$ in. long

Bottom side rails, $1\frac{1}{16}$ in. thick (before shaping) by $1\frac{5}{8}$ in. wide by $8\frac{1}{8}$ in. long

Runners, $\frac{5}{8}$ in. thick by $1\frac{3}{8}$ in. wide by $7\frac{5}{8}$ in. long

Slip tenons, $\frac{5}{16}$ in. thick by $\frac{5}{8}$ in. wide by $1\frac{1}{4}$ in. long

Splines, $\frac{3}{16}$ in. thick by $\frac{1}{2}$ in. wide, attach divider rails to runners and kickers.

Drawer sides, $\frac{3}{8}$ in. thick

Inside faces of leg taper from $1\frac{3}{8}$ in. at top to $1\frac{1}{16}$ in. at bottom

LOWER RAIL JOINT DETAIL

Lower side rail

Lower front rail

$\frac{1}{4}$ in.

$\frac{1}{2}$ in.

$\frac{3}{4}$ in.

$\frac{3}{16}$ in.

$\frac{5}{16}$ in.

$\frac{3}{16}$ in.

Leg

Legs, $1\frac{3}{4}$ in. thick by $1\frac{3}{4}$ in. wide (before shaping) by $31\frac{1}{8}$ in. long

How to Form the Gunstock Joint

Cut the miters on both parts of the joint first, but don't try to create a seamless curve until after the joint is glued together.

Start at the top of the legs. First lay out the entire leg and then create the mitered part of the gunstock joint on the inside faces. After cutting the mortises for the rails and the panels, bandsaw down from the top of the leg to the peak of the miter. Use a fence to guide the cut.

Taper the lower section. Attach the template to the leg with double-faced tape and use a bearing-guided straight bit to clean up the tapered sections. Stop ½ in. short of the gunstock joint; this area will be completed after the base is assembled.

Shape the rails. After mitering the ends of the lower rails, bandsaw the concave profile between the miters. Then clean up the surface using a template and bearing-guided bit. Again, stop just short of the gunstock joint.

Inside the Gunstock Joint

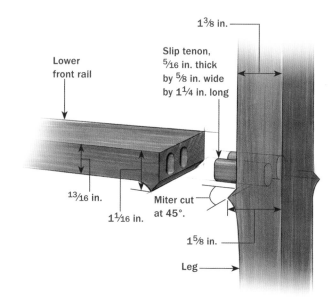

Lower front rail

1⅜ in.

Slip tenon, 5/16 in. thick by 5/8 in. wide by 1¼ in. long

13/16 in.

1¹/16 in.

Miter cut at 45°.

1⅝ in.

Leg

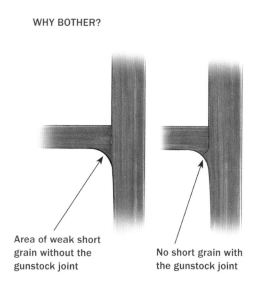

WHY BOTHER?

Area of weak short grain without the gunstock joint

No short grain with the gunstock joint

around the joint. You'll want to leave extra material here so that you can finish shaping the joint after glue-up.

Decorative chamfers and miters

Subtle chamfers surround the drawer openings and side panels, but instead of the legs and rails meeting in a normal miter, which would involve insetting the rails into the legs, they meet in a false, or mason's, miter. Begin by routing the chamfer on the inside edge of all the rails. Mark the legs where the rails intercept them, and then rout a chamfer on the legs, stopping short of this mark. The mason's miters are completed after the table is assembled because clamping pressure during glue-up may slightly change where the legs and rails meet, misaligning the chamfers.

After making the remaining parts for the base of the table, begin the assembly by gluing the sides together. Next, glue the bottom assembly and the front and back bottom rails to the runners, then glue the top

Mason's miters. The front, back, and side rails receive a decorative chamfer along their inside edges.

Another Nice Detail: Mason's Miters

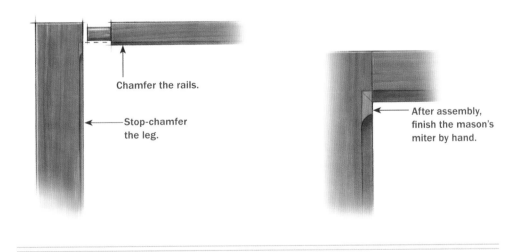

Chamfer the rails.

Stop-chamfer the leg.

After assembly, finish the mason's miter by hand.

Stop-chamfer the legs. Dry-fit the rails to the legs and lightly mark where they meet (left). Chamfer the inside corners on the show faces of the legs. Stop just short of where they intersect with the rails (above). The mason's miters will be completed after the table base is assembled.

Assemble the base in stages. Prefinish the panels completely and then glue together each side of the table (above). Glue up the top and bottom assemblies, glue the bottom assembly to the sides, insert the prefinished back panel and the drawer dividers, and then glue in the top assembly (right).

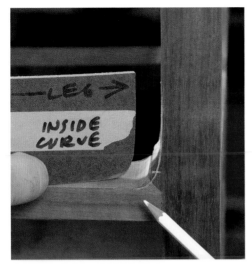

Now fair the joints. Lay out the gunstock curve. Use a template to draw the finished curve.

Shape and smooth it. A coarse Microplane® removes the waste wood quickly.

Finish the mason's miters. Create a stop cut where the rail's chamfer meets the leg; then use a plane iron to complete the chamfer on the leg.

assembly and the front and back top rails to the kickers. Glue the bottom assembly to the sides using slip tenons, then attach the top assembly via dovetailed tenons in the tops of the legs, sandwiching the partitions.

With the base glued together, you can fair the gunstock joints and complete the mason's miters. To mark the termination point of the chamfers on the legs, register a plane iron,

bevel up, against the chamfer on the rail and slice cross-grain into the leg, making sure to maintain the angle. Now register the back of the iron against the chamfer on the leg to meet the cut you just made. If you have to go against the grain, take your time, skew the iron, and make sure it is super sharp to avoid tearout.

How to inlay across solid wood

Stringing defines the field of both the table-top and the drawer fronts, adding a typical Barnsley combination of elegance and formality to the overall piece. I chose holly, not just because of its visual merits but also because it works beautifully with hand tools and you don't have to worry about the walnut dust getting in the pores and muddying the white color.

Routing the groove is easier on the table-top than the more fiddly drawers, so begin with that. Mark out the corners, then use either a plunge or a fixed-base router equipped with an edge guide to make the $\frac{1}{16}$-in.-sq. grooves, taking care not to rout past the end points. I always use a carbide down-spiral or down-shear bit (Freud® No. 04-096; www.woodcraft.com and other online sites) as the downward pressure minimizes fuzz on the top edge of the groove. As an extra precaution, I rout the groove through a strip of masking tape.

Holly Stringing Outlines the Tabletop and Drawer Fronts

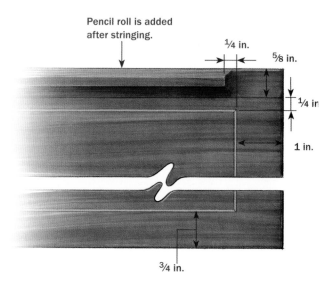

Pencil roll is added after stringing.

¼ in.

⅝ in.

¼ in.

1 in.

¾ in.

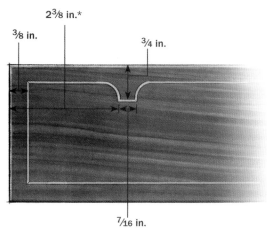

2⅜ in.*

⅜ in.

¾ in.

⁷⁄₁₆ in.

*For center drawer; changes to 4 in. for side drawers.

To be sure the holly stringing fits the groove, I make it myself. Starting with a 1×1 stick, I bandsaw 3/16-in.-thick strips. To plane them down to 1/16 in., I use double-faced tape to attach them to MDF. Last, I bandsaw them 1/8 in. wide, with a zero-clearance insert in the throat.

The top is solid walnut and will expand and contract across the grain with seasonal changes in humidity. Running long-grained stringing across the grain could cause the stringing to pop out. To avoid this, you want the stringing also to be cross-grain.

Using a block of holly about 1 in. sq., saw slices off the end as thick as the width of the groove in the tabletop. Use a plane iron and a mallet to chop these slices into five or six sections. Don't worry about getting the sizes exactly the same, because they'll be planed flushed once installed in the table. Glue these pieces edge to edge into the groove. At the corners, butt the pieces together rather than trying to miter the fragile cross-grain stringing.

For the drawer fronts, you can use a plunge router with an edge guide, except for the

Cut Clean Grooves

The combination of a down-spiral bit and masking tape minimizes tearout when cutting grooves for the stringing.

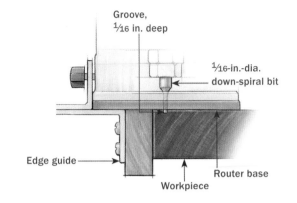

Groove,
1/16 in. deep

1/16-in.-dia.
down-spiral bit

Edge guide

Router base

Workpiece

Install the stringing. Mill the long-grained stringing to 1/16 in. thick. Use a glue syringe to inject the glue into the groove.

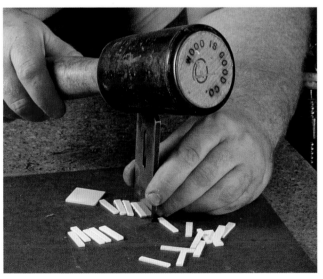

Like slicing salami. Double-faced tape on the stop block ensures you don't lose thin sections when slicing end-grain holly.

Chop the slices. Use a sharp plane iron to cut each slice of holly into five or six sections.

End grain up. The short sections of end-grain holly will move seasonally with the solid-wood tabletop.

Trim it flush. Use a scraper to bring the stringing flush with the tabletop. Near the corners, use a plane iron to avoid tearout.

curved portions near the drawer pulls. Here, use the plunge router with a template bushing and follow a Masonite® template to get the curved shape. I made a short template and moved it to each curved section, but the extra time spent lining up the template to make sure the curve flows smoothly would have been better spent making one long template.

The curve is too tight to hand-bend the stringing without breaking it, so instead use a hot pipe to soften the wood and allow it to bend.

Though some of the stringing on the drawer fronts goes cross-grain, the span is too short to need cross-grain stringing. Let the inlay dry, and then plane and scrape the holly flush. Finally, attach the tabletop.

Straight grooves first.
Use a router equipped with an edge guide to cut the grooves for the straight sections of stringing.

Make a template. A piece of Masonite attached with double-faced tape guides a bushing on the router when cutting the curved grooves adjacent to the drawer pulls. Spend some time aligning the template so the curved groove transitions perfectly into the straight sections.

Tame the Curves with Pattern Routing

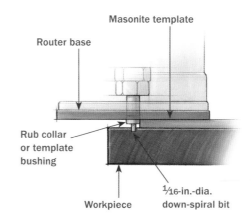

Masonite template

Router base

Rub collar or template bushing

Workpiece

1/16-in.-dia. down-spiral bit

Round the bend and miter the joints. For the curved stringing, soften and bend the holly on a piece of pipe heated with a propane torch (top). Dry-fit each section of stringing, mark the ends (above), then remove the stringing and miter the ends with a plane iron (left).

Build a Bow-Front Hall Table

CHARLES DURFEE

A simple, rectangular table can be functional and quite lovely. But give it a gentle curve along the front and you'll have a table with elegance. A subtle curve grabs attention without being loud and distracting.

The large drawer in the front apron of this table is functional without detracting from its clean look. I cut its face from the front apron, so with the drawer closed, the sweep of the apron runs uninterrupted from side to side. I also beveled the front legs, so the curve of the apron extends seamlessly across them.

Making a curved-front table isn't as hard as you might think. A single pattern can be used to make both a form for laminating the front apron and a full-size top-view drawing that helps you lay out and assemble the drawer, its guides, and the rest of the table base. I'll also show you a few very simple jigs that make it easy to crosscut the curved apron and cut tenons on its ends.

A curve has sprung. Make a pattern of the apron's curve on a piece of ¼-in.-thick MDF. Spring a batten between two brad nails spaced 51 in. apart and hold it in place with a third. Trace the curve and cut away the waste.

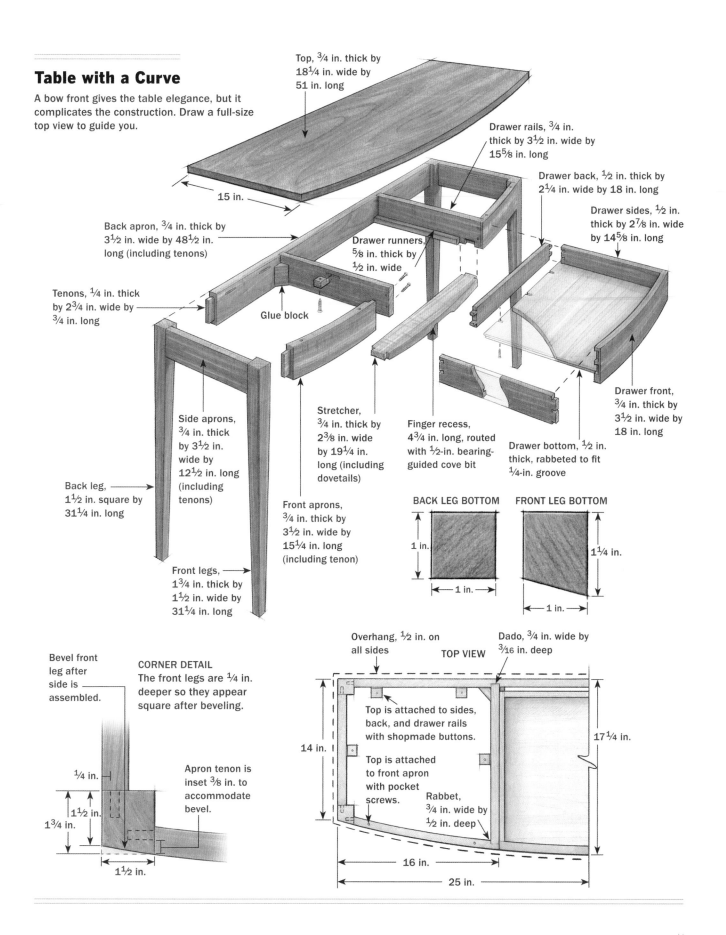

Table with a Curve

A bow front gives the table elegance, but it complicates the construction. Draw a full-size top view to guide you.

Top, 3/4 in. thick by 18 1/4 in. wide by 51 in. long

15 in.

Drawer rails, 3/4 in. thick by 3 1/2 in. wide by 15 5/8 in. long

Drawer back, 1/2 in. thick by 2 1/4 in. wide by 18 in. long

Drawer sides, 1/2 in. thick by 2 7/8 in. wide by 14 5/8 in. long

Back apron, 3/4 in. thick by 3 1/2 in. wide by 48 1/2 in. long (including tenons)

Drawer runners, 5/8 in. thick by 1/2 in. wide

Tenons, 1/4 in. thick by 2 3/4 in. wide by 3/4 in. long

Glue block

Side aprons, 3/4 in. thick by 3 1/2 in. wide by 12 1/2 in. long (including tenons)

Stretcher, 3/4 in. thick by 2 3/8 in. wide by 19 1/4 in. long (including dovetails)

Finger recess, 4 3/4 in. long, routed with 1/2-in. bearing-guided cove bit

Drawer front, 3/4 in. thick by 3 1/2 in. wide by 18 in. long

Back leg, 1 1/2 in. square by 31 1/4 in. long

Drawer bottom, 1/2 in. thick, rabbeted to fit 1/4-in. groove

Front aprons, 3/4 in. thick by 3 1/2 in. wide by 15 1/4 in. long (including tenon)

Front legs, 1 3/4 in. thick by 1 1/2 in. wide by 31 1/4 in. long

BACK LEG BOTTOM

1 in.

1 in.

FRONT LEG BOTTOM

1 1/4 in.

1 in.

Bevel front leg after side is assembled.

CORNER DETAIL
The front legs are 1/4 in. deeper so they appear square after beveling.

1/4 in.

1 1/2 in.

1 3/4 in.

Apron tenon is inset 3/8 in. to accommodate bevel.

1 1/2 in.

Overhang, 1/2 in. on all sides

Dado, 3/4 in. wide by 3/16 in. deep

TOP VIEW

Top is attached to sides, back, and drawer rails with shopmade buttons.

Top is attached to front apron with pocket screws.

Rabbet, 3/4 in. wide by 1/2 in. deep

14 in.

17 1/4 in.

16 in.

25 in.

Begin with the Curved Apron

Laminating the apron from plies cut from a single board ensures a beautiful, continuous grain pattern across the front. But the top edge of the drawer front will still look like a piece of solid lumber, a nice detail when the drawer is open.

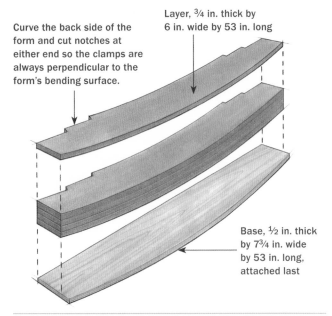

Curve the back side of the form and cut notches at either end so the clamps are always perpendicular to the form's bending surface.

Layer, ¾ in. thick by 6 in. wide by 53 in. long

Base, ½ in. thick by 7¾ in. wide by 53 in. long, attached last

Everything follows the curve

With most curved furniture, it's best to start with the curve, in this case the front apron. It's far easier to make the other parts fit the curve than to make the curve fit the other parts. I laminated the front apron rather than cutting it from solid stock, which can result in unattractive grain patterns.

To begin, make a full-size pattern of the curve. You'll use it to make the bending form for laminating the front apron and for laying out the apron and top when you do the full-size drawing. Mark, cut, and smooth the curve carefully, because the pattern affects the accuracy and beauty of everything that follows. To mark the curve, spring a flexible strip of wood, known as a batten, between two nails, but make sure the curve is symmetrical before marking it. Do this by measuring from the baseline to the curve in 5-in. increments. If

Mark the curve. Use double-faced tape to attach the pattern to a piece of ¾-in.-thick MDF. The MDF should be the same length as the pattern, but about ¼ in. wider.

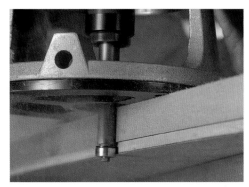

After cutting away most of the waste at the bandsaw, use a router and a flush-trimming bit to clean up the curve and shape it to the pattern. Leave about ¹⁄₁₆ in. of waste to be routed. The author uses a bottom-bearing bit and places the pattern below it. You can use a top-bearing bit if you place the pattern above.

Use the pattern to mark the remaining layers of the form and bandsaw the waste. Screw the first layer to the second and use it as a pattern to rout the second one flush. Do the same for the remaining layers.

Glue and trim the apron. Use a foam paint roller to spread an even coat of glue on mating surfaces, then stack the plies in front of the form, outside face down on the bench.

Clamp from the center out. To get even pressure and minimize creep, start in the center and work outward from side to side. Small MDF cauls under the clamp heads spread the clamping pressure.

After the glue has dried, remove the apron from the form, scrape one edge clean, and run it across the jointer.

The second edge can be cleaned and squared, and cut to width, all at once. Rip it concave side up, keeping the piece against the table at the leading edge of the blade.

the curve is symmetrical, the two measurements farthest from the center on either side will be the same, the next two farthest will be the same, and so on. If it's not symmetrical, adjust the batten and secure it with brads as needed.

Smooth the curve with a cabinetmaker's rasp, then a file, and finally a sanding block (120-grit). When smoothing the curve, work up to, but not past, the line. Hold the rasp and file diagonally across the MDF to get as much body on the surface as possible. That helps keep the curve smooth.

Full-scale drawing simplifies construction

With your pattern in hand, use it to make a full-size, top-view drawing of the table. Include the top, aprons, legs, drawer, drawer rails, and joinery details.

The front apron is cut into three parts, and the drawer rails double as stretchers to reinforce the right and left sides of the apron. Their position and length must be exact, or the table won't be square or the curve continuous. The drawing makes it a snap to get them right. It also makes assembling the table much easier.

Use a thin piece of plywood for the drawing rather than a sheet of paper. It is more durable and will make a good base for marking joinery and assembling parts.

Support blocks are the key. To get cuts parallel to the drawer's eventual sliding motion, use a support block shaped to cradle it parallel to the table. Guide it through the blade with a miter gauge and hold the offcut securely so it doesn't fall into the blade.

Trim the apron to length. A second block, shaped to match the inside of the apron, makes it possible to crosscut the front apron pieces to length and get them square.

Cut Apart the Drawer and Aprons

To give the illusion of a continuous apron, the drawer front is cut from the middle of the lamination. A support block makes it easier to cut it out accurately and to get square ends. A second block simplifies trimming and tenoning.

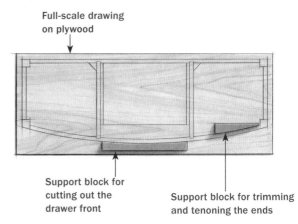

Full-scale drawing on plywood

Support block for cutting out the drawer front

Support block for trimming and tenoning the ends

Lamination without perspiration

The form isn't difficult to make. A router and flush-trimming bit ensure that when you're done, you'll have a uniform curve and a smooth surface.

A plywood base attached to the form allows you to clamp it to the bench and acts as a fence to keep the plies aligned. Cover the curved surface with packing tape to keep glue from sticking to it.

I used six plies to laminate the front apron. Leave them a few inches long so the drawer front can be cut out. I resawed them from 8/4 stock, first cutting them a bit fat and then planing them down to ⅛ in. thick. To keep the plies from being torn up by the planer, I put a long, ¾-in.-thick MDF auxiliary bed in it.

It's important to keep the plies in sequence so that the top edge of the drawer front will look clean and unified when the drawer is open. Before resawing, draw a carpenter's triangle on the edge of the board to help keep the plies in order.

To laminate the plies, I used yellow glue and applied it with a small paint roller (see the top left photo on p. 85). I know that others recommend urea-formaldehyde glue because it creeps less after drying, which prevents springback, but I've never had any problem with yellow glue. Work quickly, and stack the plies on the form as you go.

Once you have all the plies on the form, start clamping down the lamination, beginning in the middle. Use as many clamps as you can fit onto the assembly.

Leave the clamps on for 24 hours. After removing the apron from the form, scrape any glue squeeze-out from one edge and joint it. Then rip the apron to width on the tablesaw. If you don't immediately crosscut it to make the drawer front, clamp it lightly from end to end to help it keep its shape.

Make the base before the top

While you're waiting for the glue to dry, you can mill the rest of the parts, except for the top. There's no guarantee that the table base will come out precisely as planned. That could be disastrous if the top is already made, because there isn't much overhang.

Mill your parts a bit oversize and let them sit for a day or two. This allows them to release internal stresses, which can cause warping, cupping, and twisting. Then mill the parts to final dimensions.

To cut the drawer front from the apron, you'll need a support block. Bandsaw it from solid wood, and attach it to the apron with double-faced tape. The bandsawn surface needs to be smooth for the tape to stick, so smooth it like you did the pattern. I wrapped tape around both to reinforce the double-faced tape.

Cut the drawer front ⅛ in. long on each end so you can make adjustments when you fit the drawer. The amount of wood lost during fitting won't affect the grain match along the front apron, especially if you use quartersawn or rift-sawn stock.

Next, cut the apron pieces to length. Use the full-size drawing to mark their lengths accurately.

Angle the tenons, not the mortises

Cut the mortises using the method of your choice. I cut all of the mortises straight and angled the tenons on the front apron pieces, because cutting angled tenons is easier than cutting angled mortises.

After the mortises are done, cut the tenons on the side and back aprons at the tablesaw with a stack dado cutter, using a miter gauge to control the pieces.

Use the second block for tenons, too. Attach it to the apron with double-faced tape to cut the cheeks of the angled tenons (above). A shopmade tenoning jig straddles the fence and guides the workpiece through the cut (right).

On the front aprons, the tenon cheeks are cut at the tablesaw and the shoulders are cut by hand. Before you do any cutting, scribe the shoulders on the edges with a marking gauge and then use a knife to scribe across the faces. Cut the first cheek on both apron pieces. Then adjust the fence and cut the second cheek. Cut the tenons a bit thick. After the cheeks have been cut, use a backsaw to cut the shoulders, and trim the tenons to fit with a shoulder plane.

When all of the joints are cut and fit, glue the side aprons into their legs. Having the side assemblies together will make it easier to lay out the joinery for the drawer rails. Before you glue them up, however, taper the two inside faces of the legs. I did this on the tablesaw with a tapering jig, but you could do it on a bandsaw.

After the glue is dry, take the side assemblies to the jointer and bevel the front faces of the front legs.

Use the drawing to dial in the drawer pocket

Before you can attach the front and back aprons to the side assemblies, you need to cut dadoes in the back apron and rabbets on the front apron pieces to hold the drawer rails.

Those dadoes and rabbets, however, must be located precisely to get a square hole for the drawer to slide into. The best way to lay them out is by dry-fitting the front and back aprons into the side assemblies. Do this upside down on top of the full-scale drawing. The drawing will help you align all the parts square before you clamp them. You can then transfer the joint locations directly from the drawing to the aprons.

To cut the rabbets on the front apron pieces, I ran them vertically past the dado cutter. Use the support block used for cutting the tenons between the apron and the tall fence of the tenoning jig. The dadoes in the back apron are cut by guiding the apron over

Saw the shoulders by hand. There's no need to jig up and cut the shoulders at the tablesaw. A backsaw or pull saw will take care of them, and a bench hook is all you need to hold them steady.

Clean up with a shoulder plane. The author flips over his bench hook to hold the curved apron pieces for trimming the shoulders and cheeks. You'll need a chisel to get into the most acute corner.

the dado cutter with a miter gauge. At this point you also can mark the length of the drawer rails directly from the assembly and crosscut them to length.

Now is the best time to cut pocket holes in the front apron for attaching the top. These fix the front edge of the tabletop, locking in its short overhang. The seasonal movement is then transferred to the back, where the tabletop is attached to the rear apron with wooden buttons. Rout the slots to house the buttons now.

Reassemble the side assemblies and legs upside down on the drawing. Dry-fit the drawer rails to the assembly and check your results.

The next step is to cut the joinery for the stretcher that runs between the drawer rails. The stretcher is located so that there's about a 1/16-in. gap between it and the back of the drawer front. I glued a strip of cork to the stretcher to fill the gap. That way, the drawer closes with a solid, but muted, thump.

Cut the tails on the stretcher, and then transfer them to the drawer rails. I roughed out the sockets with a router and then cleaned them up with a chisel.

Sizing the parts and gluing up the table could be tricky, so do it in stages. To start, make the sides. Apply glue to the tenons and then fit the legs to the apron.

Now bevel the front legs. Use a bevel gauge and the drawing to set the jointer fence to the correct angle. Take light cuts, and use push sticks near the cutterhead.

Mark the stretcher joinery. Cut the tails on the stretcher. Then, with the rails in place, lay out the dovetail sockets.

Size the rails. After cutting the dadoes in the back apron, dry-fit the table again and clamp it down to the full-size drawing. Crosscut one end of the rail and align that end with the dado. Then mark and cut the rail to length.

The drawing guides the glue-up too

After the stretcher is fitted, finish gluing up the base. Do this on top of the drawing to ensure that everything is square and aligned properly. Before brushing on any glue, dry-fit everything and check to make sure that the table is square. If it's not, correct the problem now.

Put waxed paper between the plywood drawing and any glue joints so you don't accidentally glue them together.

After the assembly is dry, reinforce the rabbet joint connecting the drawer rails to the front aprons with screws and plug the holes. The drawer runners can just be glued in. The two long-grain glue surfaces are strong enough without reinforcement.

Tips for a curved drawer

I used traditional dovetail joinery to make the drawer, with a solid bottom that's slid in from the back.

I think a pull or knob would detract from the front's beauty, so I routed a finger recess into the stretcher that runs between the drawer rails. Use a ½-in. cove bit and a handheld router, and center the recess.

Crosscut the drawer front to fit its opening, using the same support block used to separate the drawer front from the apron.

To rout the groove for the drawer bottom in the curved drawer front, I attached the curved support block I used earlier when cutting out the drawer front. This gives a wider surface for the router base. Clamp the drawer front in a vise, and use a bearing-guided slot-cutting bit to rout the groove.

Make and attach the top

Glue up the boards and check the bottom assembly to get the correct width and length. Rip the top to width, crosscut it to length, and plane it to final thickness.

Complete the assembly. The full-size drawing keeps things square. Clamp one side to the drawing (left), glue up the back apron, and attach the other side. Use the drawing to align the parts and then clamp everything together and down to the bench (right). To keep the parts square, check their alignment with the drawing as you tighten the clamps.

Stretcher is the keystone. The last piece to glue in place is the stretcher. By bridging the drawer pocket, it keeps the table square, adds stability, and helps prevent racking.

It's important that the curve of the top matches the curve of the front apron. The curve is shallow enough that you can use the original pattern as a template and flush-trim the top to create an even overhang.

I prepped the surfaces for finishing using a smoothing plane and then a card scraper with a fine hook. I used three coats of Minwax® antique oil finish. Let each coat dry for at least 24 hours. Wet-sand the second and third coats with P320-grit paper before wiping off the excess.

Attach the top to the bottom and stand back and admire your work. Then move it into your house, where its beauty and elegance will surely be welcomed.

Simplify Dovetails on a Curved Drawer

The smartest way to cut dovetails in a curved drawer front is to flatten the curve so the sides can have straight shoulders.

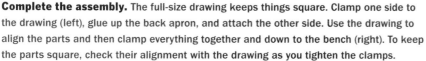

Plane here.

Tails on drawer side

Plane it flat. Mark the area to be flattened and plane away the waste. The small flats simplify the next step.

Transfer the tails. Clamp the drawer front in a vise and shim the drawer side until the tails sit flat.

Build a Hayrake Table

MICHAEL PEKOVICH

When it came time to make a new dining table, I knew I wanted it in the Arts and Crafts style, but I was also looking for a twist. For inspiration, I looked to the English countryside, the birthplace of the Arts and Crafts movement. What I found was a hayrake library table by Sidney Barnsley, one of the pioneers of English Arts and Crafts design. The table gets its name from the unique lower stretcher system, which splays out at the ends like a hayrake. I really like the table's massive timber-frame look, with its obvious through-tenons and heavy chamfers, and building it is a refreshing break from typical woodworking projects.

Another distinctive feature of the table, though it may not be apparent at first, is the orientation of the legs. They're at 45° instead of parallel to the edges of the tabletop. This makes the joinery to the hayrake stretcher simple—just a single through-mortise. Things get a little more interesting at the top.

Start with the Legs

The through-mortise at the bottom is standard, so we'll focus on the diagonal joinery at the top.

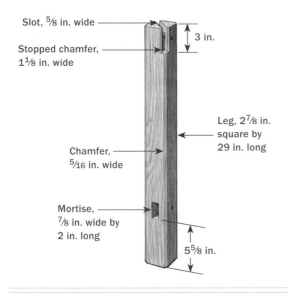

Slot, $5/8$ in. wide

Stopped chamfer, $1^1/8$ in. wide

3 in.

Chamfer, $5/16$ in. wide

Leg, $2^7/8$ in. square by 29 in. long

Mortise, $7/8$ in. wide by 2 in. long

$5^5/8$ in.

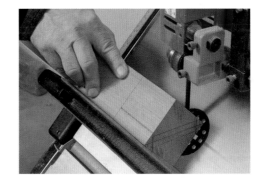

Cut the stopped chamfer. Bandsaw then handsaw. Tilt the bandsaw table to 45° and cut the flats (top). Clamp the leg in a vise and use a handsaw to cut the shoulders (above). Then clean up the sawn surfaces with a shoulder plane and chisel.

Anatomy of a Hayrake Table

Thick stock, through-tenons, and heavy chamfers add timber-frame charm. Use rift-sawn stock for the legs and stretcher to get straight grain lines on all the faces of the parts.

*Note: On dimensions marked with an asterisk, exact lengths of parts will be determined during the construction process.

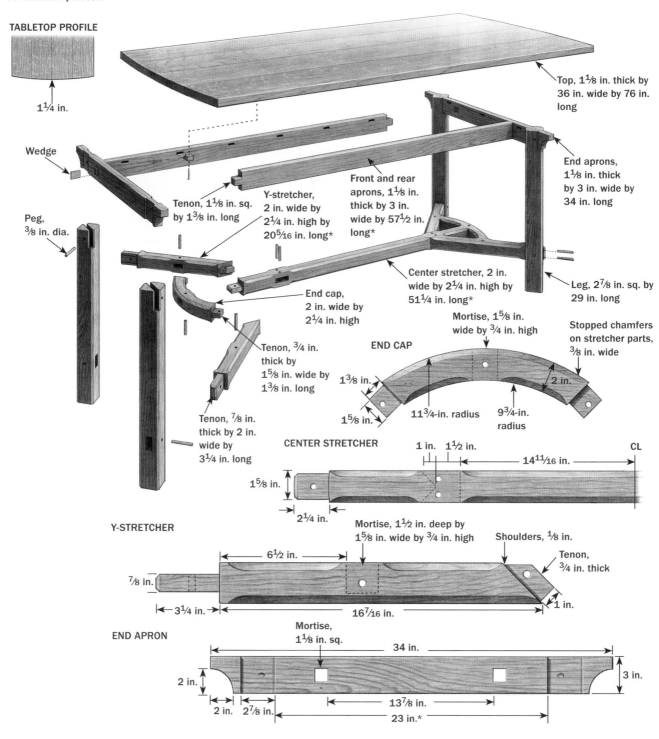

TABLETOP PROFILE

1 1/4 in.

Top, 1 1/8 in. thick by 36 in. wide by 76 in. long

Wedge

Tenon, 1 1/8 in. sq. by 1 3/8 in. long

Y-stretcher, 2 in. wide by 2 1/4 in. high by 20 5/16 in. long*

Front and rear aprons, 1 1/8 in. thick by 3 in. wide by 57 1/2 in. long*

End aprons, 1 1/8 in. thick by 3 in. wide by 34 in. long

Peg, 3/8 in. dia.

End cap, 2 in. wide by 2 1/4 in. high

Center stretcher, 2 in. wide by 2 1/4 in. high by 51 1/4 in. long*

Leg, 2 7/8 in. sq. by 29 in. long

Tenon, 3/4 in. thick by 1 5/8 in. wide by 1 3/8 in. long

Mortise, 1 5/8 in. wide by 3/4 in. high

Stopped chamfers on stretcher parts, 3/8 in. wide

END CAP

1 3/8 in.

1 5/8 in.

11 3/4-in. radius

9 3/4-in. radius

2 in.

Tenon, 7/8 in. thick by 2 in. wide by 3 1/4 in. long

CENTER STRETCHER

1 5/8 in.

2 1/4 in.

1 in.   1 1/2 in.

14 11/16 in.

CL

Y-STRETCHER

Mortise, 1 1/2 in. deep by 1 5/8 in. wide by 3/4 in. high

Shoulders, 1/8 in.

Tenon, 3/4 in. thick

7/8 in.

6 1/2 in.

3 1/4 in.

16 7/16 in.

1 in.

END APRON

Mortise, 1 1/8 in. sq.

34 in.

2 in.

3 in.

2 in.   2 7/8 in.

13 7/8 in.

23 in.*

Then cut the slot. Saw, drill, chisel. With the bandsaw table still tilted to 45°, cut one side of the slot, rotate the leg, and cut the other side (above). This ensures a perfectly centered slot. Now make a 45° cradle to hold the leg, and drill a hole at the bottom of the saw cuts to remove the waste (top right). Finish up with a chisel (bottom right).

Each pair of legs is connected with end aprons that slot into their tops. This requires a slot cut diagonally across the top of the leg as well as a wider stopped chamfer. It looks like a tricky joint, but a bandsaw simplifies the task.

How to get thick stock

The base of this white-oak table requires 12/4 stock. If you can find it, buy rift-sawn stock for straight grain lines on all the faces. If you can't find these massive planks, you can get by with 8/4. Here's how. Reduce the thickness of the hayrake stretcher parts just 1/8 in., to 1 7/8 in., and glue up the 2 7/8-in.-thick leg stock from two 1 1/2-in.-thick layers. Make sure the layers are flatsawn so the glueline will be hidden in the straight grain lines on the edges. Mill all the parts to final width and thickness but leave all the stretcher pieces about 1 in. extralong at this point.

Now you can launch into the stocky joinery, walking in the footsteps of timber framers past. The legs are the place to start. Cut out the stopped chamfer at the top of the

leg and then create the slot. When the lower mortise on the leg is complete, chamfer the corners on the tablesaw.

Rake section is easier than it looks

The lower stretcher system is where the fun begins. The curved and angled parts look daunting, but if you tackle the joinery one step at a time, it's really not that tough. The curved end cap actually simplifies the joinery.

Join the Y

Now it's time to tackle the hayrake stretcher. The stretcher array gives the table its farmhouse flair, but the angled stretchers and curved cap on each end also present the biggest joinery challenge of the project. Breaking down the construction into simple steps is the key to success.

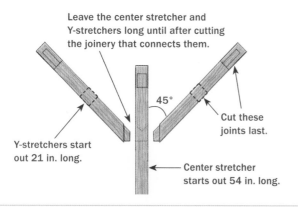

Leave the center stretcher and Y-stretchers long until after cutting the joinery that connects them.

45°

Cut these joints last.

Y-stretchers start out 21 in. long.

Center stretcher starts out 54 in. long.

Make the angled mortises. Start by cutting a through-mortise in the center stretcher. To create the 45° angled shoulders, clamp a 45° block in place to use as a guide (above). Chop out a bit at a time until the chisel is resting on the block (left).

It allows you to cut mortises in the angled Y-stretchers at 90° instead of 45°.

The first task is to join the Y-stretchers to the center stretcher. The ends eventually will be tenoned to fit the end caps, but leave the stretcher long for now, taking all measurements from its midpoint. Start by cutting the through-mortises, noting that one shoulder on each side is cut at 45° to receive the diagonal stretchers. Cut a simple through-mortise, then chop the angled shoulder with a chisel.

With the mortises done, tenon the Y-stretchers. Finally, use a backsaw to cut the tenon ends and clean them up with a block plane.

With the angled tenons done, it's quick work to cut the stretchers to length and tenon the ends to fit the leg mortises. While you're at it, bandsaw kerfs in the tenons for wedges. The last task is to cut the mortises that the end cap goes into.

Now the angled tenons. Leave the stretchers long and miter one end using an angle guide on a tablesaw sled (1). Install a dado blade and adjust your miter gauge so the end of the piece is flush with the rip fence, and cut the tenon (2). You'll have to readjust the gauge for the opposite face, but the rip fence can stay put. Last, trim a triangle off the end to fit the angled mortise (3). Once the angled end is done, cut the stretcher to length, tenon the opposite end, and finally cut the mortise for the end cap.

How to handle the curved end cap

The final component of the hayrake stretcher is the end cap itself. Its construction is pretty simple because the joinery is cut while the stock is square.

Miter the ends of the end cap on the tablesaw, then tenon the ends. Set the end cap against a miter gauge and adjust the angle until the mitered end is flush with the rip fence, then cut the cheeks with a dado blade. Now locate the tenon ends using a scrap block as shown on p. 99.

Next, you'll mortise for the center stretcher and cut the end cap to shape. Lay out the curves as shown, but bandsaw out some of the waste on the inside face to make mortising easier. Cut the curved profile on

End Cap: Cut the Tenons before the Curves

The end cap starts as a block with mitered ends. All of the joinery is cut at a 45° angle, which the tablesaw and bandsaw handle easily.

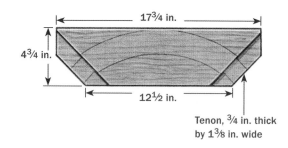

17¾ in.

4¾ in.

12½ in.

Tenon, ¾ in. thick by 1⅜ in. wide

More angled shoulders. Start by mitering the ends of the end cap on the tablesaw using the same sled you used for the Y-stretcher ends. This will ensure an exact angle match between all of the joints. Then cut the tenon cheeks with a dado blade as before (above).

the bandsaw and clean up with a block plane and spokeshave. A spindle sander or sanding drum mounted in a drill press also works well for the inside face. With the end cap shaped, tenon the center stretcher and cut it to length (see the photos on p. 100).

Drawbore pins replace clamps

It would be difficult to get clamps on this odd-shaped stretcher assembly for gluing. So I created a self-clamping joint using drawbore pegs. It looks like a simple pegged joint, but the holes in the parts are slightly offset so that when the peg is driven in, it pulls the joint together tightly. I also added wedges in most of the through-tenons. They add extra strength and also close any visible gaps. I don't angle the mortises, but just kerf the tenons, drive in thin wedges, and trim them flush.

Smart methods for thick chamfers

The last task before assembly is to chamfer the parts. These chamfers were originally made by hand with a drawknife. I wanted to keep the handmade look, but I speeded things up by using a router for most of the work. The trick is to rout the chamfer, stop short of the end lines, and then use a chisel to finish it. This way, the chamfer flows from part to part.

I find it easiest to dry-fit the parts and rout the chamfers as a unit. I use a light touch and rout in the climb-cut direction to avoid tearout. As long as you don't take too heavy a pass, the router won't get away from you. Stay well away from intersections.

After routing the top and bottom faces of the stretcher assembly, mark the joint intersections and disassemble the parts. Use a chisel to complete the chamfer. Small irregularities are a good thing, but avoid chiseling deeper than the routed chamfer.

Lay out the tenons. Dry-fit the Y-stretchers to a mortised scrap block. Then place the end cap over the stretchers, sliding it forward until its shoulders are snug. Use a square to mark the mortise locations on the ends of the tenons.

Cut the tenon ends on the bandsaw. Use a miter gauge to guide the workpiece, flipping it backward in its slot.

Scrap Block Is the Secret

A mortised block allows you to assemble the Y-stretchers and mark the end-cap tenons and curve without the long center stretcher getting in the way.

Scrap block

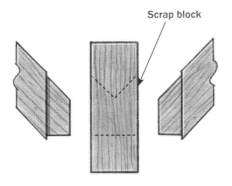

Now cut the curve. Dry-fit the end cap to the assembly and lay out its curves (above right). After sawing out the center of the end cap so you can mortise for the center stretcher tenon, cut the curves on the bandsaw (right).

Center stretcher is the final piece. Use the complete end cap to scribe the shoulders on the center rail and cut it to length. Leaving the center rail long until now is key to a gap-free assembly. To scribe the curved tenon shoulders, dry-fit the stretchers and clamp on blocks even with the end-cap mortises.

The end cap is now elevated, which lets you align it with the mortises so you can scribe the shoulder accurately on the center rail. To mark the bottom, extend the scribe marks down the rail sides, flip the rail and align the end cap to the marks, and scribe.

Cut a square shoulder, then pare to fit. Cut the tenon with a dado blade, stopping short of the curved shoulder. Then use a chisel to pare to the scribe line.

All together now. All of the pieces come together at once, bit by bit. When fine-tuning the fit, keep in mind that the top face of the stretcher is most critical. Feel free to flip it to put the best side up.

Get ready for glue-up

I make my own pegs, ripping stock to ⅜ in. square and then pounding it through a dowel plate (www.lie-nielsen.com). I cut the pegs long and taper the leading end with a pencil sharpener so that it can clear the offset holes. I lightly chamfer the top of the pegs because they are left slightly proud of the surface. To ensure a consistent peg height, I drill a shallow hole in the end grain of a scrap block and position it over the peg when driving it in.

Assembly begins by gluing up the hayrake stretcher. When both ends are assembled, flip the stretcher over and trim the bottoms of the pegs flush. With the stretcher glued up, dry-fit the legs and measure for the upper stretcher frame. Because of all the odd angles, it's better to take dimensions from the workpiece rather than from a set of plans. Start by measuring between the legs to locate the bridle joints on the end aprons. Cut the bridle on the tablesaw with a dado blade. Then cut the corbel profiles on the ends and mortise for the front and rear aprons. Fit the end aprons in place and measure between them to determine the shoulder-to-shoulder length of the long aprons.

Offset Pins Take the Place of Clamps

The angled and curved parts of the hayrake stretcher are nearly impossible to clamp for glue-up. Instead, drawbore pegs driven into intentionally misaligned holes pull the joints together tightly. It's a time-tested method for both assembling and reinforcing joinery.

By offsetting the tenon peg holes slightly toward the shoulder, the mortised joint will be drawn tight as the peg is driven in.

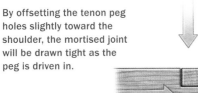

Tenon hole is offset.

1/32 in.

Drill through the mortised parts. Insert a scrap into the mortise to prevent blowout inside.

Mark and drill the tenon. With the holes drilled, dry-fit the parts again and insert the drill bit into each peg hole, giving it a twist to mark the center point (1). Disassemble the parts and mark a new center point 1/32 in. toward the shoulder of the tenon from the drill-bit mark (2). Insert a piece of scrap below the tenon to prevent blowout when drilling (3).

Assemble from the stretcher up. Wipe a thin coat of shellac on the end grain of the through-tenons to prevent glue from soaking in. Let it dry, then glue and assemble the parts one end at a time. Start the pegs in the hole and gradually drive them in until the joints are fully seated. Then drive them all the way home.

Assemble the rest of the base. Start by gluing the legs to the hayrake stretcher, but don't drive in the wedges just yet. Before you do that, it's important to install the upper aprons to help square up the entire assembly. Then drive wedges into the through-tenons in the legs, and peg the upper frame joints.

Tenon the long aprons, then rout slots for the wooden buttons that secure the top. Finally, glue up the apron frame and drive wedges into its through-tenons. Assemble the rest of the base as shown.

Keep the color light

English Arts and Crafts furniture tends to be lighter in color than Stickley-style furniture. So, even though I fumed the white oak with ammonia, I didn't fume it as long as I normally do, just a couple of hours. I also used the weaker janitorial-strength ammonia instead of the industrial-strength. The result was a nice golden tone. I warmed it up further by wiping on a thin coat of garnet shellac before finishing with Waterlox, a tung oil–based wiping varnish.

The top is attached with buttons. The tabletop won't be attached to the base until after finishing, but the author predrills for the buttons now.

Dining Table with Two-Way Drawers

STEPHEN HAMMER

Many of my favorite designs began with a challenging request from a client, as did this table. The client wanted a dining table that would double as a worktable with a lot of storage, so I added double-fronted drawers accessible from either side. That required a drawer with half-blind dovetails at both ends and a support system that could handle the extra stress of deep drawers when fully loaded. So I designed a table with upper and lower drawer stretchers that have the vertical dividers mortised in solidly. In addition, I wanted a clean design that would tie into the eclectic setting that would be its home. I chose walnut because the table would be paired with a set of walnut Nakashima benches.

The table has the usual parts: legs, stretchers, dividers, runners and kickers, aprons, and drawers. But because it is built like a torsion box and the drawers have double fronts, the how-to is more like a cross between a chest of drawers and a basic table. Keep track of the joinery and work in the right order, and you'll have no trouble reproducing this versatile dining table.

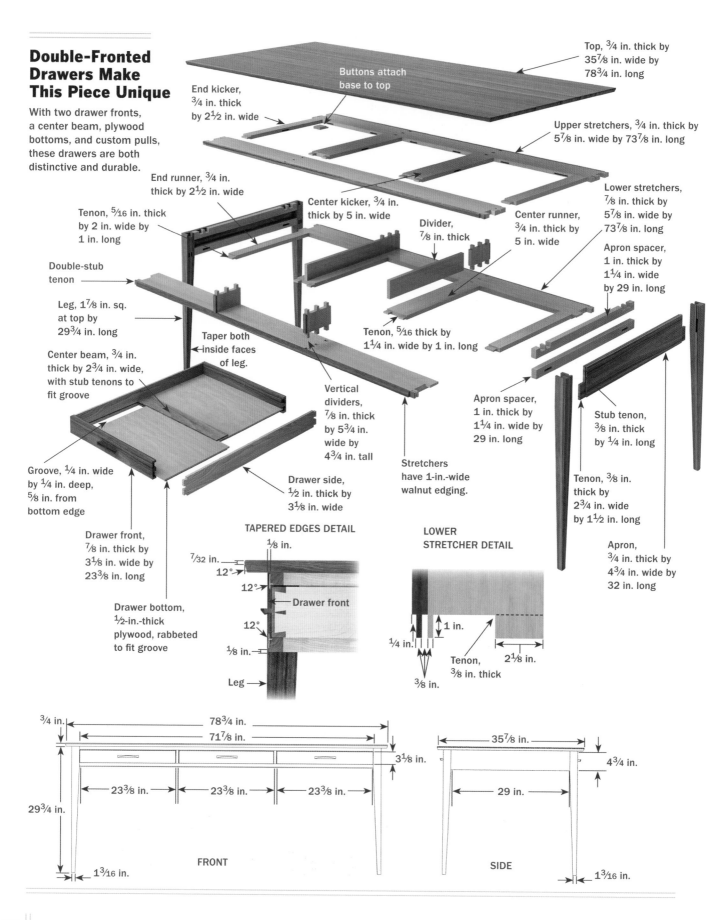

Double-Fronted Drawers Make This Piece Unique

With two drawer fronts, a center beam, plywood bottoms, and custom pulls, these drawers are both distinctive and durable.

Top, $\frac{3}{4}$ in. thick by $35\frac{7}{8}$ in. wide by $78\frac{3}{4}$ in. long

Buttons attach base to top

End kicker, $\frac{3}{4}$ in. thick by $2\frac{1}{2}$ in. wide

Upper stretchers, $\frac{3}{4}$ in. thick by $5\frac{7}{8}$ in. wide by $73\frac{7}{8}$ in. long

End runner, $\frac{3}{4}$ in. thick by $2\frac{1}{2}$ in. wide

Center kicker, $\frac{3}{4}$ in. thick by 5 in. wide

Divider, $\frac{7}{8}$ in. thick

Center runner, $\frac{3}{4}$ in. thick by 5 in. wide

Lower stretchers, $\frac{7}{8}$ in. thick by $5\frac{7}{8}$ in. wide by $73\frac{7}{8}$ in. long

Tenon, $\frac{5}{16}$ in. thick by 2 in. wide by 1 in. long

Double-stub tenon

Apron spacer, 1 in. thick by $1\frac{1}{4}$ in. wide by 29 in. long

Leg, $1\frac{7}{8}$ in. sq. at top by $29\frac{3}{4}$ in. long

Taper both inside faces of leg.

Tenon, $\frac{5}{16}$ thick by $1\frac{1}{4}$ in. wide by 1 in. long

Center beam, $\frac{3}{4}$ in. thick by $2\frac{3}{4}$ in. wide, with stub tenons to fit groove

Vertical dividers, $\frac{7}{8}$ in. thick by $5\frac{3}{4}$ in. wide by $4\frac{3}{4}$ in. tall

Apron spacer, 1 in. thick by $1\frac{1}{4}$ in. wide by 29 in. long

Stub tenon, $\frac{3}{8}$ in. thick by $\frac{1}{4}$ in. long

Tenon, $\frac{3}{8}$ in. thick by $2\frac{3}{4}$ in. wide by $1\frac{1}{2}$ in. long

Groove, $\frac{1}{4}$ in. wide by $\frac{1}{4}$ in. deep, $\frac{5}{8}$ in. from bottom edge

Drawer side, $\frac{1}{2}$ in. thick by $3\frac{1}{8}$ in. wide

Stretchers have 1-in.-wide walnut edging.

Apron, $\frac{3}{4}$ in. thick by $4\frac{3}{4}$ in. wide by 32 in. long

Drawer front, $\frac{7}{8}$ in. thick by $3\frac{1}{8}$ in. wide by $23\frac{3}{8}$ in. long

TAPERED EDGES DETAIL

$\frac{1}{8}$ in.

$\frac{7}{32}$ in.

12°

12°

Drawer front

12°

$\frac{1}{8}$ in.

Leg

Drawer bottom, $\frac{1}{2}$-in.-thick plywood, rabbeted to fit groove

LOWER STRETCHER DETAIL

1 in.

$\frac{1}{4}$ in.

Tenon, $\frac{3}{8}$ in. thick

$2\frac{1}{8}$ in.

$\frac{3}{8}$ in.

$\frac{3}{4}$ in.

$78\frac{3}{4}$ in.

$71\frac{7}{8}$ in.

$3\frac{1}{8}$ in.

$35\frac{7}{8}$ in.

$4\frac{3}{4}$ in.

$23\frac{3}{8}$ in.

$23\frac{3}{8}$ in.

$23\frac{3}{8}$ in.

29 in.

$29\frac{3}{4}$ in.

$1\frac{3}{16}$ in.

FRONT

SIDE

$1\frac{3}{16}$ in.

Lots of mortises are the key to construction

To begin, I mortise the legs and stretchers on my hollow-chisel mortiser, about 52 mortises in all. The upper and lower stretchers are mortised through their faces for the vertical dividers that separate the drawers. Take care that all these mortises line up top to bottom—their alignment is critical or the vertical dividers will be crooked. To do this, I clamp all four pieces together and, using my square as a guide, score a line across the inside edge of the stretchers. Then I transfer those lines across the faces of the stretchers to lay out the mortise locations.

Keep in mind that the legs are designed with a very simple double-sided taper that begins at the base of the apron. I cut the joinery before tapering the leg, so I can work on it while it is still flat and square. I cut the mortises for the lower stretcher and the haunched mortises for the side aprons. The upper stretchers connect to the legs with lap dovetails. The socket for the dovetail is cut later.

Now that the mortises are cut, it's time to move on to the tenons on the aprons, the drawer runners and kickers, the lower stretchers, and the vertical dividers.

The side aprons have haunched tenons, which are cut with several passes on the tablesaw with a ½-in. dado set. I lay the boards flat on the table and crosscut, using the fence to set the tenon length. The tenons on the runners and kickers are cut using the same method. To keep from interfering with the vertical drawer divider joinery, the center runners and kickers have two tenons. I remove the waste between the tenons on the tablesaw with the same sled and method I use for the vertical dividers, below. This isn't necessary on the end runners and kickers.

The tenons on the lower stretchers aren't as straightforward. They are joined with a double-stub tenon into the leg and a single tenon into the lower apron spacer. I cut the stub tenons on

Make Short Work of Multitenon Joints

The bulk of the joinery is mortise-and-tenon joints. The most challenging ones are the multiple tenons on each vertical drawer divider. Here's how to tackle them successfully.

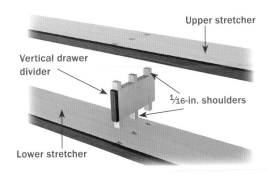

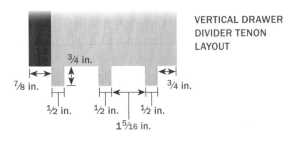

VERTICAL DRAWER DIVIDER TENON LAYOUT

Mortises first. Mark the upper and lower stretchers for the location of the vertical drawer dividers and then cut these through-mortises with a hollow-chisel mortiser, using a backer board to prevent blowout.

  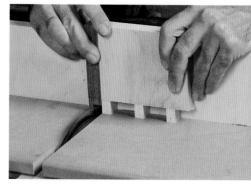

Before cutting the tenons, skim 1/16 in. of material from the tenon cheeks with a dado set. This gives a clean edge where the tenons end.

Mortises locate tenons. Use the mortises on the stretchers to locate and mark the tenons on the vertical dividers.

A very basic sled holds the vertical dividers as the waste between tenons is removed. Work carefully to lay out lines without using a stop.

the bandsaw and use the router table and a straight bit to create the tenon that lands in the spacer. I measure for the mortise in the lower apron spacer and cut it. Later, when the legs are glued to the apron, I dry-fit the lower stretcher system to the legs and apron, setting the apron spacer in place. It automatically registers itself, which allows me to mark its location and glue it in place.

Upper stretchers get dovetails

While the lower stretchers have mortises and tenons, the upper stretchers are connected to the leg and apron spacer with dovetails. This makes assembly easier. I use a simple jig to establish the sides of the tails on the bandsaw, and then I cope out the waste and clean up with a chisel. These structural dovetails are never seen, so appearance is not critical.

With all the leg joinery completed, I now feel comfortable cutting the leg tapers. With only four legs to do, I mark the taper on the legs, cut it freehand on the bandsaw, and clean it up on the jointer, making sure to register one side against the fence to keep the taper square. Later, after the legs are glued to the aprons, I'll mark and cut the dovetail socket in the top of the leg post, using a plunge router freehand. Then I clean it up with chisels.

Simplify glue-up

Because there are so many parts in the drawer system, this glue-up is more complicated than the average table glue-up. But you can break it into manageable stages: the leg/apron assembly and then the stretcher assembly. Before glue-up, do a final sanding

Wait to Do the Upper Stretchers

Unlike the lower stretchers, the upper stretchers get dovetailed into the legs and apron spacers. The quirk in the process is this: Because the dovetail sockets go partially into the apron spacers, they can't be laid out and cut until after the legs are glued to the aprons.

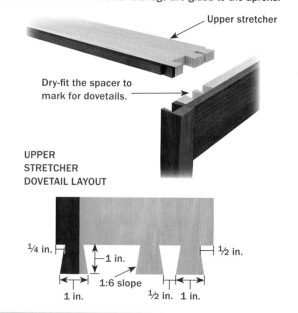

Upper stretcher

Dry-fit the spacer to mark for dovetails.

UPPER STRETCHER DOVETAIL LAYOUT

1/4 in.　　1 in.　　1:6 slope　　1 in.　　1/2 in.　　1/2 in.　　1 in.

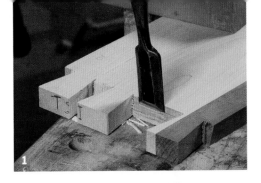

Dovetail the stretcher and lay out the sockets.
Saw and chop the dovetails and clean to the line
with a chisel (1). Dry-fit the apron spacers into
the apron/leg assembly and mark the dovetail
locations in the leg and spacer (2).

Remove the spacers to notch them. Using the tablesaw sled
again, this time with an angled fence, the author makes the cuts
to form the sides of the dovetail sockets. Then he runs the spacers
through the same dado setup but on a 90° sled to remove any
waste in the center.

Create the sockets in the legs. The author
clamps the leg-and-apron assembly into his end
vise with the top of the leg flush with the top of
the bench (4). With the router base sitting on
the bench, he routs close to the layout line, then
cleans to the line with a chisel (5).

and finishing of the table parts. I use a finely
set smoothing plane to remove millmarks,
followed by a random-orbit sander up to
P320-grit sandpaper. Then I apply Tried &
True original wood finish to all the parts. I
can always sand more after assembly, but this
step saves time, gives a nicer finish, and helps
a lot with glue cleanup.

Attach the aprons to the legs

Gluing the apron to the front and back legs is
straightforward, and the mortises dictate the
alignment of the parts. The side aprons have
upper and lower spacers glued to them that
allow the drawers to clear the legs, which are
thicker than the aprons. However, I do not
attach and cut the joinery in these spacers until
the legs are glued to the aprons. It is easier to
cut the joinery when they are separated from
the apron, but I need the leg/apron assembly
together to mark the exact location of the
joinery on the spacers. With the joinery done,
the spacers can be glued in place.

Glue in the spacers. Clamp the apron spacers into the leg-to-apron assembly.

Create two frames. The two lower stretchers are connected by the drawer runners. The two upper stretchers are connected by the kickers.

Add the lower frame to the legs. One long clamp on each side is enough to pull it all together.

Drop the vertical dividers in place and top it off. With the vertical dividers glued into the lower stretchers, you can dry-fit the top stretcher assembly until the vertical dividers are set, and then glue the top assembly in place. Or use glue with a longer open time and do it all at once.

Two sets of stretcher frames

Putting together the stretcher frames can get a little complicated (but just a little). I glue up the front and back lower stretchers with the drawer runners as one frame, then the front and back upper stretchers with the drawer kickers as a second frame.

Put it all together

Next, glue the vertical drawer dividers into the lower stretcher frame. To make sure they stay straight as they dry, use a slow-dry glue and work on gluing the upper stretcher assembly right away, or take the pressure off the glue-up and simply dry-fit the top in place until the dividers are dry.

Make Handsome Handles

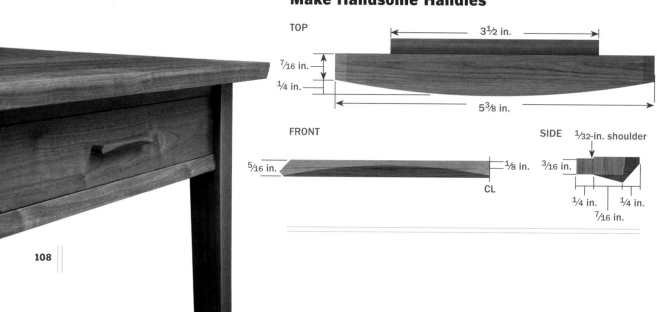

TOP

$3\frac{1}{2}$ in.

$\frac{7}{16}$ in.
$\frac{1}{4}$ in.

$5\frac{3}{8}$ in.

FRONT

$\frac{5}{16}$ in.

$\frac{1}{8}$ in.
CL

SIDE $\frac{1}{32}$-in. shoulder

$\frac{3}{16}$ in.

$\frac{1}{4}$ in. $\frac{1}{4}$ in.
$\frac{7}{16}$ in.

The final steps happen all at once. Glue the lower stretcher assembly into the leg/apron assemblies and drop the top stretcher assembly into place over the dovetail sockets and drawer divider tenons. It is critical that you check all the parts for square. Measuring the diagonals works well for this. Here you also can just dry-fit the top in place while the bottom stretcher dries and then add the top.

Quick and easy drawer construction

With the base assembled, it is time to focus on the drawers. I combine power tools and handwork to create consistent dovetails efficiently while keeping a hand-cut appearance. I use quartersawn white oak for the drawer sides. Its hardness lets the drawer slide easily and with little wear. It also contrasts with the walnut to show off the dovetails. Custom walnut handles are the finishing touch. By the way, I didn't use a catch to register these drawers.

Top it off

With the base complete, you can make the top. I made mine from a series of boards picked for grain appearance and glued up side by side using biscuits for alignment. After cutting the top to final size, I shaped the edge with a 12° bevel that matches the bevel on the stretchers. Wooden buttons secure the top to the frame.

To finish the top, I use a finely set smoothing plane to take out the millmarks, and then sand it up to P320-grit. I apply several coats of Tried & True original wood finish wiped on and rubbed off by hand. All parts were prefinished, but I go over the entire piece again with a final few coats.

Rip tricks. The first two rip cuts form the tenon (top). Leaving the angled cheek cut for last lets the handle stock fall away from the blade (bottom).

A few crosscuts. Multiple crosscut passes waste away material to create the tenons. Then raise and angle the blade to cut the handles to length.

Final shape. Using the tenons to secure the handles in a vise, do the shaping with a block plane.

The Versatile Trestle Table

GARY ROGOWSKI

With a simple form that allows many variations, the trestle table can look contemporary or classic. The trestles, the stretcher that joins them, and even the top can be shaped in myriad ways. The design offers easy access for diners, with no table apron to knock a knee against and more chair room on each side. And it is expandable, scaling up easily from this kitchen-size table to a large dining table.

A key feature on many trestle tables, including this one, is the wedged joinery for the stretcher, which is rock-solid even though it's called "knockdown." With a through-mortise-and-tenon joint, the stretcher locates and holds the trestles upright. In a marvel of engineering, the wedges lock everything together, preventing the table from racking along its length. I know of no stronger joint. It's also good looking: The projecting tenons and the wedges add another design element.

With this project, I'll focus on the stretcher joinery—the most challenging aspect of the project. Executing the joinery successfully relies on careful fitting of the through-tenons and the wedges to their respective mortises.

Modern Trestle Table

The trestle design is centuries old, yet its rock-solid construction and easy access for sitting remain unequaled. It can be made in any size—from breakfast to banquet table—and its wedged through-tenons let you break down the base for easy transport. What's more, it is a designer's playground, with the feet, posts, stretcher, through-tenons, wedges, and tabletop each offering room for interpretation. I like this smallish version, sized to be a desk or a kitchen table for four.

¼ in.
½ in.

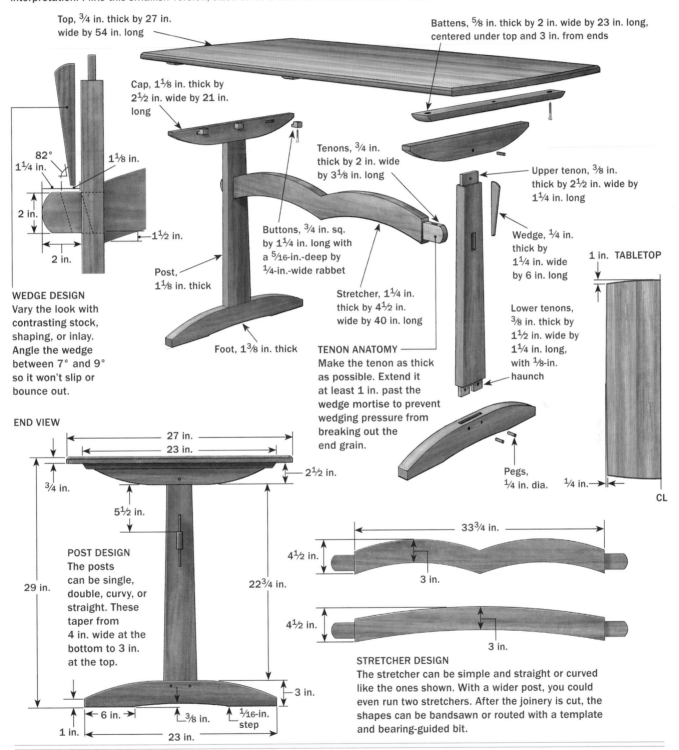

Top, ¾ in. thick by 27 in. wide by 54 in. long

Battens, ⅝ in. thick by 2 in. wide by 23 in. long, centered under top and 3 in. from ends

Cap, 1⅛ in. thick by 2½ in. wide by 21 in. long

Tenons, ¾ in. thick by 2 in. wide by 3⅛ in. long

Upper tenon, ⅜ in. thick by 2½ in. wide by 1¼ in. long

82°
1¼ in.
1⅛ in.
2 in.
1½ in.
2 in.

Buttons, ¾ in. sq. by 1¼ in. long with a ⁵⁄₁₆-in.-deep by ¼-in.-wide rabbet

Wedge, ¼ in. thick by 1¼ in. wide by 6 in. long

1 in. TABLETOP

Post, 1⅛ in. thick

Lower tenons, ⅜ in. thick by 1½ in. wide by 1¼ in. long, with ⅛-in. haunch

WEDGE DESIGN
Vary the look with contrasting stock, shaping, or inlay. Angle the wedge between 7° and 9° so it won't slip or bounce out.

Foot, 1⅜ in. thick

Stretcher, 1¼ in. thick by 4½ in. wide by 40 in. long

TENON ANATOMY
Make the tenon as thick as possible. Extend it at least 1 in. past the wedge mortise to prevent wedging pressure from breaking out the end grain.

Pegs, ¼ in. dia.

¼ in.

CL

END VIEW

27 in.
23 in.
2½ in.
¾ in.
5½ in.
29 in.
22¾ in.
3 in.
1 in.
6 in.
⅜ in.
¹⁄₁₆-in. step
23 in.

POST DESIGN
The posts can be single, double, curvy, or straight. These taper from 4 in. wide at the bottom to 3 in. at the top.

33¾ in.
4½ in.
3 in.
4½ in.
3 in.

STRETCHER DESIGN
The stretcher can be simple and straight or curved like the ones shown. With a wider post, you could even run two stretchers. After the joinery is cut, the shapes can be bandsawn or routed with a template and bearing-guided bit.

Rout the Through-Mortises

A simple template, used with a guide bushing, makes it easy to cut through-mortises to the right size, in the right place.

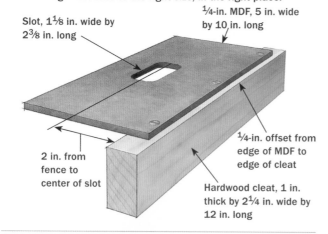

Slot, $1\frac{1}{8}$ in. wide by $2\frac{3}{8}$ in. long

$\frac{1}{4}$-in. MDF, 5 in. wide by 10 in. long

2 in. from fence to center of slot

$\frac{1}{4}$-in. offset from edge of MDF to edge of cleat

Hardwood cleat, 1 in. thick by $2\frac{1}{4}$ in. wide by 12 in. long

How to make the template. Drill a hole in the MDF, then move to the router table. The jig's cleat rides the table's fence, so the slot is cut parallel to the cleat. Start the router bit in the drilled hole and go from there. Reposition the fence for a second pass and a bigger mortise.

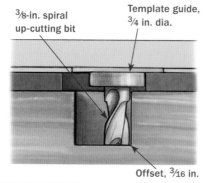

Offset the layout. The template slot is bigger than the mortise, so make a separate registration mark to locate the template accurately and carry that mark around to the other side.

Template Guide

A guide bushing rides the template's rim and shields it from the spinning bit. Be sure to factor in the bushing diameter when sizing the slot in the template.

$\frac{3}{8}$-in. spiral up-cutting bit

Template guide, $\frac{3}{4}$ in. dia.

Offset, $\frac{3}{16}$ in.

How to cut large, clean mortises

Furniture construction is like painting a floor. Careful planning keeps you out of the corners. In this case, it's important to lay out and cut the large through-mortises in the posts before shaping the posts to preserve a parallel reference edge for guiding the router.

I use a template guide bushing and a simple shopmade mortising jig to rout mortises. The jig consists of a $\frac{1}{4}$-in. MDF routing template attached to a fence that registers against the stock. The jig centers the mortises on the width of the posts, but you'll still need to do a little layout. First, measure from the top of each post to mark the tops and bottoms of the mortises. Use a square to carry the lines around to the board's opposite face, then check the edges of both boards side by side to ensure that the marks line up. Then, because the jig's slot is slightly larger than the mortise itself, make a separate registration mark to locate the jig accurately.

Clamp the mortising template securely in place on the outside face of the post. To cut the mortises, I use a plunge router and a $\frac{3}{8}$-in. spiral-fluted bit. It's possible to rout all the way through the post or stop short of full

Rout the mortise. With the template in place, cut halfway through the stock. Then flip the board end for end (right) to ensure that the jig is clamped to the same reference edge for the second cut.

depth and clear the remaining waste with a chisel. But for a technique that will work for posts of greater thickness, start by routing away—in shallow passes—about half of the mortise depth. Then remove the template, flip the workpiece, reattach the template on the opposite face, and finish the cut.

After routing the mortises, chop them out square, working in from both faces. Now you can shape those posts.

Cutting tenons on a long board

The size of the stretcher makes it generally difficult to handle. For example, it's too long to support safely in a tablesaw tenoning jig. Whatever tenoning method you use, it needs to be clean and accurate—all the more so because the tenon's fit will be visible where it exits the big through-mortise.

As with the big posts, joinery comes before shaping. After laying out the stretcher shape and tenon location, I cut the shoulders on the tablesaw, using a miter gauge with a long fence or a crosscut sled with a long stop-block attachment to hold the work and locate the cut. To cut the tenon cheeks, I use the bandsaw with a roller stand for

Clean up with a sharp chisel. Chop the corners square, working in from both faces.

infeed support and a 6-tpi blade for a smooth surface.

Before cutting the tenon to width (height), I clean up the cheek cuts, trimming the tenon to the proper thickness. To keep the cheeks flat near the shoulder, I use a shoulder plane, but I'll switch to a block plane for quicker stock removal near the tenon ends. Remember that the last 2 in. or so of the

Cut the shoulders on the tablesaw. Use a miter gauge with a long fence or a crosscut sled to manage the long stock.

Move to the bandsaw. Use a test cut to adjust the fence for drift. Leave the cheeks slightly fat for trimming and cleanup.

Clean up the cheeks. Plane away the sawmarks and adjust the fit. Use a shoulder plane to get into the corners.

Cut the tenon to width. Again, leave the tenon slightly oversize. Make the adjoining cut with a handsaw to remove the waste.

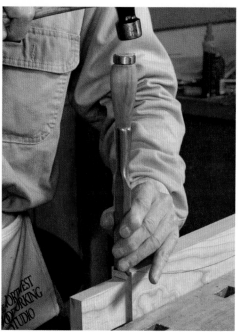

Clean up the shoulder. Using the tablesawn shoulders as a reference, walk the chisel's edge across the hand-sawn section to establish your line, then chop away the waste.

tenon won't be housed in the assembled joint, so that section can have a slightly looser fit.

I also cut the tenon to width on the bandsaw, again leaving it just oversize and cleaning up with hand tools until it slides through the mortise with no gaps showing on the outside face.

The wedge mortises

The last step in making the tenon is to create the mortise for the wedge. In addition to cutting the mortise straight through the entire width of the tenon, the trick here lies in cutting the outer end of the mortise at an 8° angle. The secret is that the inside wall of

the mortise is buried in the post and doesn't need to be chopped out square, so you can cut the entire mortise at 8° on the drill press. If your drill press doesn't have a tilting table, use a jig like the one shown in "Drill the Wedge Mortises" on the facing page.

Mark out the wedge mortise with a centerline in the tenon thickness. Mark the

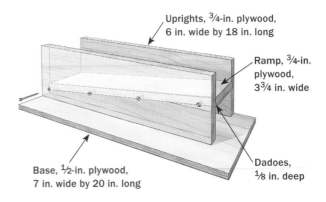

Drill the Wedge Mortises

The author built this simple jig to secure the stretcher at an 8° angle for drilling out the wedge mortises. The jig clamps to the drill-press table and the work is clamped to the jig.

Uprights, ¾-in. plywood, 6 in. wide by 18 in. long

Ramp, ¾-in. plywood, 3¾ in. wide

Base, ½-in. plywood, 7 in. wide by 20 in. long

Dadoes, ⅛ in. deep

Position the jig. The jig stays put on the drill-press table. Slide the workpiece in the jig to reposition it, and clamp it in place for each new hole.

mortise end at ¾ in. past the post, but have it start ⅜ in. inside the post. In this way, the wedge won't bottom out against the back side of the mortise. Using a brad-point bit, drill the holes at each end of the mortise first. Work slowly and clear out the waste often. Then drill out the middle section. To chop out the remaining waste, clamp the stretcher

Support the cut. Place a block underneath the tenon to prevent blowout where the drill bit exits the cut.

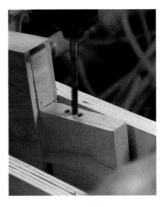

Start at the ends. Where holes overlap, make sure the bit's centering point hits wood so it locates properly.

Layout line is a visual reference. Mark the angle on the tenon's cheek and sight down the line while chopping away the waste.

Cut the wedges and assemble. The bandsaw is safer than the tablesaw. The author uses a simple jig made of ³⁄₈-in. MDF with an 8° notch cut into it.

Tap the wedges home. When the wedges are tightly driven, they pull the tenon shoulders firmly against the post for an assembly that won't budge.

on the bench and use layout lines on the tenon at the 8° angle or a sliding bevel placed on the bench to sight against for chopping. Chop in toward the center of the mortise from both the top and bottom, flipping the workpiece as needed. Chamfer the wedge mortise on both top and bottom so the wedge slides through more easily.

I cut the wedges on the bandsaw using a simple holding jig. Set a sliding bevel to the angle of the mortise and mark out the shape of the wedge on a piece of ¼-in. MDF. Carefully cut out that shape and file the edges straight. Glue another piece of MDF to the bottom of this template to hold the workpiece in place. Make up wedge stock at the proper thickness and length and at roughly the correct width. Then set the bandsaw fence to cut out the wedge. Clean up the wedges with a bench plane, holding them in a vise or in the jig on a shooting board.

Shaker Dining Table

CHRISTIAN BECKSVOORT

This table is based on a piece built at the Shaker community in Hancock, Mass. (It's now in the collection of the Fruitlands Museum in Harvard, Mass.) The original, made from cherry, is almost 11 ft. long, with a third trestle to support the center. Such a length made good sense for communal dining, but it's not practical for most homes today. My version has only two trestles, and I typically make the top either 8 ft. or 9 ft. long.

A trestle table has appeal for a few reasons. For one, it can be knocked down without fuss. Remove the top from the base parts and the stretcher from the trestles, and you can move the table through doors and up or down stairs. Unlike most tables, which have aprons around the perimeter to stiffen the structure, trestle tables have a single center stretcher. This gives more vertical legroom. On the other hand, most trestle tables have flat feet, which tend to get in the way of the feet of diners sitting at either end. This Shaker design solves that inconvenience by replacing the flat feet with arched feet. This simple change not only makes the piece more ergonomic but also gives it an especially graceful look.

Trestle Table

Lightly sand all exposed corners (except for the foot chamfers) to a ⅛-in. radius. For maximum strength, use straight-grained, defect-free wood for the feet.

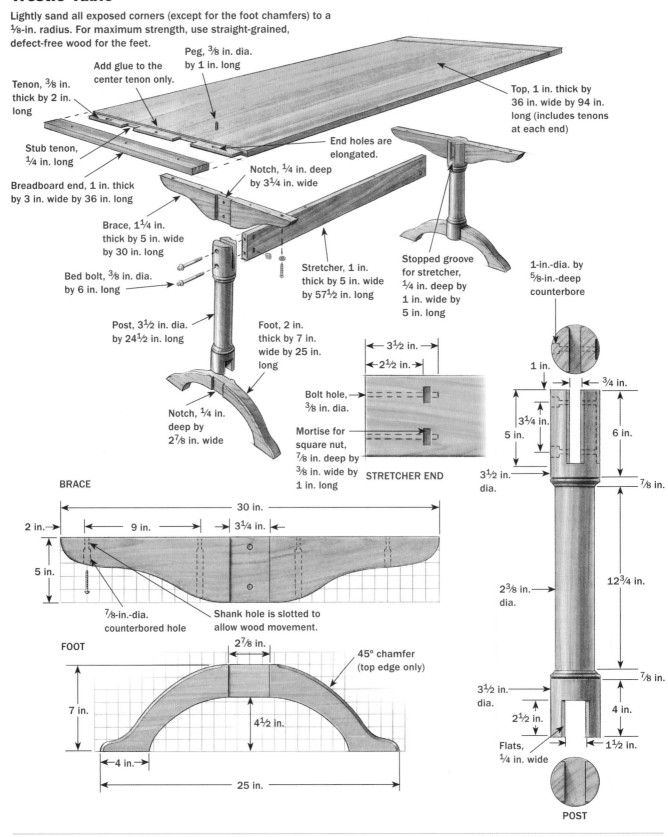

Peg, ⅜ in. dia. by 1 in. long

Add glue to the center tenon only.

Tenon, ⅜ in. thick by 2 in. long

Top, 1 in. thick by 36 in. wide by 94 in. long (includes tenons at each end)

Stub tenon, ¼ in. long

End holes are elongated.

Breadboard end, 1 in. thick by 3 in. wide by 36 in. long

Notch, ¼ in. deep by 3¼ in. wide

Brace, 1¼ in. thick by 5 in. wide by 30 in. long

Bed bolt, ⅜ in. dia. by 6 in. long

Stretcher, 1 in. thick by 5 in. wide by 57½ in. long

Stopped groove for stretcher, ¼ in. deep by 1 in. wide by 5 in. long

1-in.-dia. by ⅝-in.-deep counterbore

Post, 3½ in. dia. by 24½ in. long

Foot, 2 in. thick by 7 in. wide by 25 in. long

Notch, ¼ in. deep by 2⅞ in. wide

Bolt hole, ⅜ in. dia.

Mortise for square nut, ⅞ in. deep by ⅜ in. wide by 1 in. long

STRETCHER END

3½ in.

2½ in.

1 in.

¾ in.

3¼ in.

5 in.

6 in.

3½ in. dia.

⅞ in.

BRACE

30 in.

2 in.

9 in.

3¼ in.

5 in.

⅞-in.-dia. counterbored hole

Shank hole is slotted to allow wood movement.

2⅜ in. dia.

12¾ in.

FOOT

2⅞ in.

45° chamfer (top edge only)

7 in.

4½ in.

4 in.

25 in.

3½ in. dia.

2½ in.

⅞ in.

Flats, ¼ in. wide

1½ in.

POST

The posts are simple turnings. The author turns a 3⅝-in.-sq. blank to 3½ in. dia., then makes a series of 2⅜-in.-dia. parting cuts along the midsection, checking the diameter with calipers. After that, with the parting cuts serving as guides, he reduces the entire midsection to 2⅜ in. dia.

Each end of the midsection terminates in a cove and bead. Mark the ⅞-in. width of the detail by lightly touching a pencil point against the spinning post. Cut the cove with a roundnose chisel or small gouge, then the bead with a diamond-point or skew chisel.

Most lathes will handle these posts

I make the posts first, using 16/4 stock. If this size isn't readily available, consider face-gluing two pieces of 8/4 stock from the same board. Using the same board means the grain and color of the pieces will be close and the glue joint less visible.

Mill the stock to about 3⅝ in. sq. and crosscut it to 24½ in. long. Then mount it in a lathe and turn it to 3½ in. dia. At a point 6 in. from the top and 4 in. from the bottom, use a parting tool and calipers to establish the 2⅜-in. dia. of the center section.

Continue using the parting tool to make a series of 2⅜-in.-dia. cuts between the end cuts. With these cuts serving as a depth guide, use a gouge to reduce the entire center section to 2⅜ in. dia. At each end of the center section, turn a small cove and a bead with a small flat at each end of it (see "Coves and Beads" at right). If your turning skills are rusty, practice first on a shorter blank.

Jig simplifies post joinery

Once both posts are turned and sanded, they need to be notched for the braces, feet, and stretchers. To hold them for layout and machining, I clamp the posts to a shopmade cradle that consists of a couple of U-shaped saddles screwed to a rectangular piece of

Coves and Beads

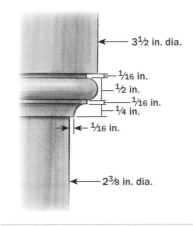

3½ in. dia.

1/16 in.
½ in.
1/16 in.
¼ in.
1/16 in.

2⅜ in. dia.

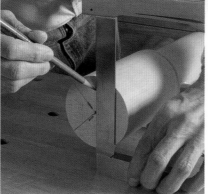

Build a cradle. Two saddles screwed to a base, ¾ in. thick by 8 in. wide by 12½ in. long, create a cradle for the post.

Lay out the location of the notches. With the cradle on a flat surface, use a square to mark a vertical centerline on each end of the post (left). Measure and mark the width of the notch, then use a square to scribe the notch depth (right).

Cut the two notches. With the post securely clamped in the cradle, use a bandsaw to cut the notch on each end, following your layout lines by eye.

plywood. A narrow piece of paper towel in each saddle, held in place with masking tape, helps prevent scratches on the posts.

Place the cradle on a bench (with the clamp between the opened jaws of the vise so the cradle can rest flat). Use a square to lay out the width and length of the notch on each end of the post. To lay out a notch, first use a square to mark a vertical line through the center of the turning. Using that centerline as a reference, mark the width of the notch. Finally, mark the depth of the notch. The notches can be cut by hand with a deep backsaw, but a bandsaw does as good a job in less time. With the post clamped in the cradle, carefully saw between the lines to the bottom of the notch. Then nibble out the bottom of the notch with the blade. As you

switch from one end to another, you'll need to reposition the clamp so it doesn't bump into the saw table as you cut.

Rout a shallow groove for the stretcher

There's one more machine cut to make on each post—a groove, ¼ in. deep by 1 in. wide by 5 in. long, that will accept the end of the stretcher. You can cut the groove with a chisel, but it's easier on a router table.

Again, I use the cradle to support the post. A clamp gets in the way on the router table, so I made a wooden yoke that serves as a clamp. With the yoke screwed to the base of the cradle, the post stays securely in place. Before tightening the yoke, make sure the cheeks of the slot are parallel with the router-table surface.

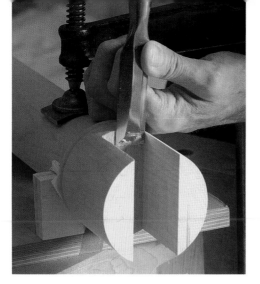

Cut small shoulders. Cut a flat on each side of the notches to ensure a gap-free contact between the post and the brace and foot. First, lay out each flat with a pencil and ruler (left), then make a vertical cut with a chisel to establish the end point. Finally, make horizontal cuts with the chisel to pare the stock to the layout line (below).

Hand work. Smooth the ends of the notches and the cheeks with a sharp chisel.

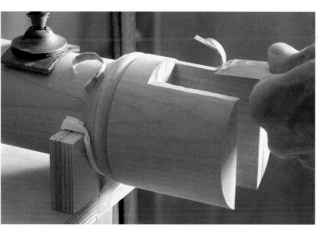

Install a 1-in.-dia. straight bit in the router and raise the bit to make a ¼-in.-deep cut in the post. Adjust the router-table fence so that when the cradle slides against it, the bit is centered on the post. Also, clamp a stop block to the fence to stop the cradle when the groove is 5 in. long. Hold the cradle firmly against the fence as you slide it forward to feed the post in the bit.

The router bit leaves rounded corners at the end of each groove. Use a chisel to cut them square.

Fit the other parts to the posts

Templates for the brace and feet can be found on p. 118, but you'll need to enlarge them to full size. I'm not fussy about pattern stock; light cardboard or poster paper works just fine.

Use the patterns and a pencil to transfer the profiles to the stock. Cut the parts on the bandsaw, staying just outside the lines. Next, lay out and mark the location of the dadoes in the braces and feet. These mate with the deep notches in the posts. They can be cut by hand, with a router, or with a dado blade on the tablesaw. To save time, I use the dado blade set for the widest possible cut.

To support the braces and feet during the dado cuts, clamp a long fence to the miter

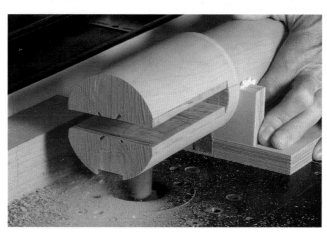

Cut the groove for the stretcher. With a U-shaped yoke screwed to the cradle serving as a clamp, use a router table to cut a stopped groove in the top end of the post (above). Square the rounded end left by the router bit with a chisel (left).

Complete the trestles. To dado the legs and braces, cut a wide dado on each side of the brace and foot. Use the tablesaw miter gauge with a long auxiliary fence to support the parts during the cuts. A pair of stop blocks helps ensure that the ends of the dadoes end up perfectly aligned.

Dry-fit the parts. Check the fit of the posts to each dado (top). If it's too tight, use a rabbet plane to trim the sides or bottom of the dado (above).

gauge. The fence should extend at least 15 in. on either side of the dado blade. Add a pair of stop blocks to ensure that the shoulders of the dadoes align perfectly on both sides of the joint. When setting the depth of cut, I leave the areas between the dadoes a bit thick. That way, I can trim them with a rabbet plane for a perfect final fit.

With the dadoes cut, I smooth the concave edges of the braces and feet using a spindle sander and the convex edges using a stationary disk sander. Smooth the curved edges further by hand-sanding.

Now use the router table and a chamfer bit to rout a ¼-in. chamfer along the top edges of the feet. Stop each chamfer at a point ½ in. from the dadoes.

To fit a joint, first make a knife cut at the shoulders of the dado to sever the wood fibers before trimming the dadoes with a rabbet plane. When the joint begins to engage, I mark the leading edges of the slots with a pencil, which shows me exactly where the joint is still tight. A few more strokes with the rabbet plane and the joint should fit snugly.

Once all braces and feet are fitted to their respective posts, the parts can be glued and clamped to create a trestle. A pair of clamps, each spanning from brace to foot, is all that's

Rout chamfers. A chamfer bit in a router table is used to chamfer the top edges of the feet. Stop the cut ½ in. short of the dado.

Add the bed bolts. Start by drilling. With a trestle clamped in the cradle and the cradle clamped to the drill-press table, use a 1-in.-dia. Forstner bit to drill a ⅝-in.-deep hole (shown). Then, remove the Forstner bit and use a ⅜-in.-dia. brad-point bit to drill a hole completely through the post.

needed. After that, at one end of the trestle, measure the distance from the top edge of the brace to the bottom edge of the foot. Do the same at the other end. The measurement should be the same. If they differ, adjust the pressure on the two clamps until the measurements agree. Once dry, sand the bottom of the post and the underside of the arched foot until flush.

When making the stretcher, I start with slightly thicker stock. Then I make light passes with a thickness planer until the stretcher fits snugly in the groove routed in the top of the post.

How to install bed bolts

Each trestle attaches to an end of the stretcher with a pair of ⅜-in. by 6-in. bed bolts and nuts (available from Horton Brasses; www.horton-brasses.com). Each bolt extends through a post and brace and into the end of the stretcher. The end of the bolt threads through a nut mortised into the stretcher. When the bolt and nut are tightened, the stretcher and trestle are pulled together to produce a rock-solid joint.

The bed-bolt work starts at the drill press. Once again, the cradle comes in handy. Use the yoke to secure the trestle to the cradle, with the stretcher groove facing down. Make

Drill holes in the ends of the stretcher. Add a trestle to the stretcher temporarily, then use a ⅜-in.-dia. brad-point bit to extend the bed-bolt hole slightly into the end of the stretcher. After that, remove the trestle and drill deeper to complete the hole.

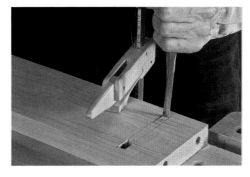

Lay out the location of the bed-bolt nuts. With a bed bolt in a stretcher hole serving as a guide (in case the hole isn't drilled perfectly square), mark the location of the bed-bolt nut (top). Cut the mortises for the nuts just deep enough to allow the bolt to thread into the nut (above).

Put it together. After all the parts have been sanded and finished, it's finally time to put the table together. With the table parts upside down, slide the ends of the stretcher into the post grooves and slip the bed-bolt nuts into the mortises in the stretcher (left). Then insert the bolts (above).

Attach the top. A screw and washer go into each counterbored hole in the braces. The slotted shank hole allows for wood movement.

sure the sides of the brace and trestle are parallel to the work surface. If the parts tilt, the holes won't be square.

Measuring from the top end of the post, mark the hole centers at 1 in. and 4¼ in. Position the cradle so that a 1-in. Forstner bit is centered on the upper hole. Clamp the cradle to the drill press, and then bore a ⅝-in.-deep hole to accept the head of the bed bolt. Replace the Forstner bit with a ⅜-in.-dia. brad-point bit and bore a hole completely through the post and brace. Repeat the process for the remaining holes.

Next, clamp the stretcher in a vise and temporarily mount one of the trestles. Transfer

the ⅜-in.-dia. bit from the drill press to a portable drill. Using the holes in the trestle as guides, drill matching holes in the end of the stretcher. Remove the trestle and continue drilling until the hole is at least 3½ in. deep, measured from the end of the stretcher.

Portable drills rarely produce a hole perfectly square to the stretcher ends. So to make sure the mortise for the nut is properly located, I use a bed bolt as a guide. Allow a good portion of the bolt to extend from the hole. Then place a long ruler so it's centered along the length of the exposed bolt. Use a pencil to extend the centerline along the face of the stretcher. With the centerline showing the location of the bolt hole, measure 2½ in. from the end of the stretcher, and lay out the location of the mortise for the nut. A few minutes' work with a chisel yields a mortise just big enough to accept the nut. You'll know the alignment is OK if you can slip the bolt into the hole and thread it into the nut. I use a special bed-bolt wrench (available from Horton Brasses; a 12-point socket also works) to turn and tighten the bolts.

With the holes drilled and all the mortises cut, you can mount the trestles to the stretcher.

Build the top and breadboard ends

I make the tabletop by edge-gluing 1-in.-thick stock, using three or four well-matched boards across the 36-in. width.

Breadboards are applied to either end. The original table, made from ⅞-in.-thick stock, had a ¼-in.-thick by ½-in.-long tongue cut fully across each end of the top and pinned to allow for wood movement. The tongue fit into a corresponding groove cut across the entire length of the breadboard end. I make my tenons longer for added strength.

The top is attached with screws driven through counterbored holes in the braces and stretcher. To allow the top to expand and contract in width due to seasonal changes in humidity, be sure to elongate the shank holes in the braces.

For a finish, I use an oil-and-varnish mix (equal parts of each), applying three coats to all the table surfaces, including the top and bottom of the top and breadboard ends. For added durability, the top then gets two more coats.

Form meets function in this classic table design.

A Revolution in Chair Making

MICHAEL C. FORTUNE

I have designed dozens of chairs during my career and have made several hundred. Whenever I design one, I strive to make it beautiful, comfortable, and strong. Meeting those goals often means the chairs are difficult to build, with parts meeting at compound angles. And then all those parts must be hand-shaped so they join seamlessly.

Thus I began looking for a less complex way to make chairs, while remaining true to my design goals of beauty, comfort, and strength. In traditional chair making, the legs, rails, seat, and back are part of a single unit, which complicates construction quickly. With this design, I borrowed from techniques developed in Scandinavia during the mid-20th century. By separating the seat and back from the legs and rails, you build the chair's base first and then add the seat and back to it. As a result, the legs and rails can be square to one another, which simplifies the joinery. But the seat and back can be highly contoured for comfort and then attached to the base with screws (I have a great technique for the shaping).

A chair like this is for a dining table, so you'll be planning to make at least four, but more likely six or eight. Because you're basically taking your woodworking into production mode, I'll show you some nifty jigs that will make the process go more smoothly and quickly.

Ultimate Jig for Slip Tenons

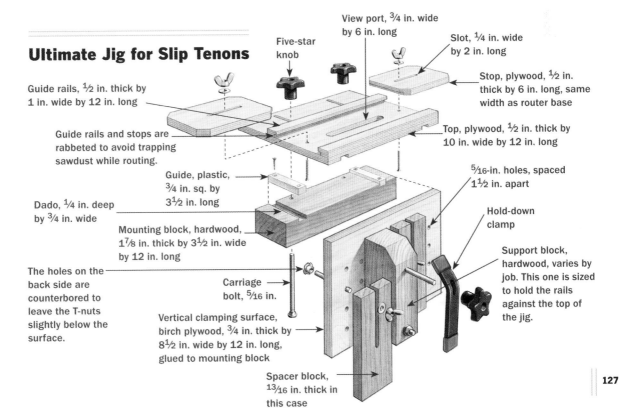

View port, ¾ in. wide by 6 in. long

Five-star knob

Slot, ¼ in. wide by 2 in. long

Stop, plywood, ½ in. thick by 6 in. long, same width as router base

Guide rails, ½ in. thick by 1 in. wide by 12 in. long

Guide rails and stops are rabbeted to avoid trapping sawdust while routing.

Top, plywood, ½ in. thick by 10 in. wide by 12 in. long

⁵⁄₁₆-in. holes, spaced 1½ in. apart

Guide, plastic, ¾ in. sq. by 3½ in. long

Dado, ¼ in. deep by ¾ in. wide

Hold-down clamp

Mounting block, hardwood, 1⅞ in. thick by 3½ in. wide by 12 in. long

Support block, hardwood, varies by job. This one is sized to hold the rails against the top of the jig.

The holes on the back side are counterbored to leave the T-nuts slightly below the surface.

Carriage bolt, ⁵⁄₁₆ in.

Vertical clamping surface, birch plywood, ¾ in. thick by 8½ in. wide by 12 in. long, glued to mounting block

Spacer block, 1³⁄₁₆ in. thick in this case

Square Frame Meets Comfy Curves

All the joints in this chair are straight, so it's much less difficult to make than most others. Add the author's clever approach to the curved parts, and a full set of six or eight is within the reach of first-time chair makers.

FRONT LEG

$1\frac{7}{8}$ in.

$\frac{3}{4}$-in. radius

$1\frac{1}{4}$ in.

$\frac{1}{2}$ in.

$1\frac{3}{8}$ in.

$1\frac{5}{8}$ in.

$1\frac{1}{8}$ in.

$\frac{7}{8}$ in.

BACK LEG

18°

$\frac{5}{8}$ in.

$\frac{3}{8}$ in.

$3\frac{1}{8}$ in.

$2\frac{3}{4}$ in.

13 in.

10 in.

$\frac{7}{8}$ in.

Seat, $1\frac{1}{8}$ in. thick by $21\frac{1}{4}$ in. wide by $17\frac{7}{16}$ in. deep

Back, 1 in. thick by 19 in. wide by 8 in. tall

Tapered plugs

Screws hold the back and seat to the chair.

Wedges

Back leg, $\frac{7}{8}$ in. thick by $2\frac{1}{4}$ in. wide by $30\frac{3}{8}$ in. long

Back rail, $\frac{7}{8}$ in. thick by $2\frac{1}{2}$ in. wide by 8 in. long

Cleat, $\frac{7}{8}$ in. square by 8 in. long

Double tenon, $\frac{3}{8}$ in. thick by $2\frac{3}{4}$ in. wide by $1\frac{5}{8}$ in. long

Side rail, $\frac{7}{8}$ in. thick by $3\frac{7}{8}$ in. wide by $16\frac{1}{4}$ in. long

Front rail, $\frac{7}{8}$ in. thick by $2\frac{7}{8}$ in. wide by 15 in. long

Slip tenon, $\frac{3}{8}$ in. thick by $1\frac{5}{8}$ in. wide by $2\frac{1}{4}$ in. long

Slip tenons, $\frac{5}{16}$ in. thick by $\frac{5}{8}$ in. wide by 2 in. long

Front leg, $1\frac{1}{4}$ in. thick by $1\frac{7}{8}$ in. wide by $17\frac{5}{8}$ in. long

DOUBLE MORTISE DETAIL

1 in.

$\frac{5}{16}$ in.

$\frac{1}{2}$ in.

$\frac{5}{8}$ in.

BACK RAIL

$34\frac{3}{4}$-in. radius

FRONT RAIL

$\frac{3}{8}$ in.

1 in.

$34\frac{3}{4}$-in. radius

$1\frac{1}{8}$ in.

$1\frac{5}{8}$ in.

$\frac{3}{16}$ in.

$2\frac{3}{4}$ in.

SEAT

$\frac{13}{16}$ in.

34-in. radius (top and front edge of seat)

29-in. radius (bottom of seat)

$\frac{5}{8}$ in.

$1\frac{5}{16}$ in.

$1\frac{1}{8}$ in.

BACK

15-in. radius (back/outside)

16-in. radius (front/inside)

1 in.

$1\frac{3}{4}$ in.

1 in.

7°

$1\frac{1}{8}$ dia.

$2\frac{1}{8}$ in. dia.

SIDE RAIL

$\frac{7}{8}$ in.

$\frac{3}{8}$ in.

$2\frac{3}{4}$ in.

$\frac{1}{2}$ in.

$\frac{3}{4}$ in.

$1\frac{3}{8}$ in.

$\frac{5}{8}$ in.

$\frac{1}{4}$ in.

$2\frac{15}{16}$ in.

$\frac{3}{8}$ in.

Lock the top of the jig. Then clamp the workpiece in place and rout the bottom mortise.

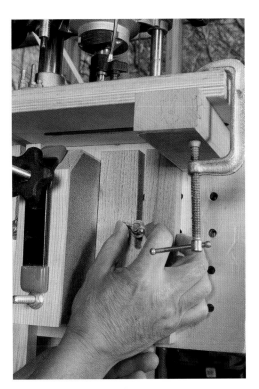

Space out for the second mortise. The spacer lets you keep the overall setup locked in and ready for the next workpiece.

I've now made a lot of chairs this way, and I couldn't be happier with the results. The basic structure and technique is flexible enough to accommodate a variety of designs. Best of all, even a novice chair maker can use the technique and make great chairs right away.

One jig handles many mortises

The curved legs give the chair an air of complexity. But that's an illusion. The rails and legs meet at right angles and slip tenons hold them together, except for an integral tenon where the side rail joins the back leg. Making the joinery comes down to routing a bunch of straight mortises. The slip tenons

Rout the Double Mortises

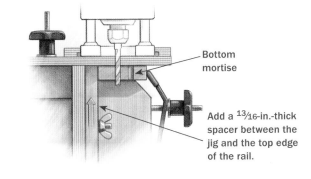

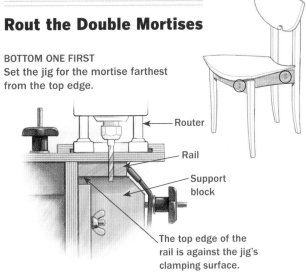

BOTTOM ONE FIRST
Set the jig for the mortise farthest from the top edge.

Router

Rail

Support block

The top edge of the rail is against the jig's clamping surface.

NOW ADD A SPACER
This lets you cut the top mortise without changing your setup.

Bottom mortise

Add a $^{13}/_{16}$-in.-thick spacer between the jig and the top edge of the rail.

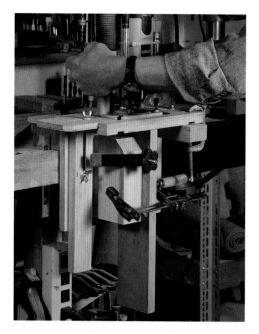

End grain mortises mount vertically. Rout the ends of the rails with the workpiece clamped against the support block, which stays exactly where it was when you were routing the face-grain mortises.

are basically straight sticks planed to fit. As for the curves in the legs, don't sweat them. Use the drawings to get you close and trust your eyes when making templates.

While the legs and rails are still straight and square, but before routing the mortises, drill holes in the back legs and side rails for attaching the back and seat.

I rout all the mortises with the help of one shopmade jig, starting with the double mortises that join the side rails to the front rail. These are oriented horizontally because vertical mortises cut across too much grain and weaken the rails. The double mortises are laid out so that the ones in the face grain and the ones in the end grain can be routed with a single setup on the jig (and a $\frac{5}{16}$-in.-dia., two-flute aluminum cutting end mill). The secret is a spacer.

Cut the Stepped Mortise and Tenon

Had the author used a slip tenon here, the mortise in the end grain of the rail would have been too close to the double mortises for the back rail, weakening the side rail.

7/8 in.

2 3/4 in.

5/8 in.

STEP 1: ROUT THE LONG MORTISE

Router

Stops control the mortise length.

3/8-in.-dia. two-flute aluminum cutting end mill

Mortise

STEP 2: ROUT THE THROUGH-MORTISES

Stop blocks are in same location.

1/4-in.-dia. two-flute aluminum cutting end mill

Through-mortise

Spacer block

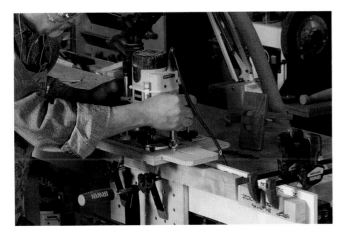

Mortise the back legs. The author adds a long piece of plywood behind the vertical clamping surface, notching it to fit around the jig's mounting block, so he can use a stop block to locate all of the legs quickly (a big time-saver when making six or eight chairs).

Another spacer to the rescue. When routing the two through-mortises in the back leg, the author puts a small block in the jig to lock in their length. He switches it to the other end of the jig for the second mortise.

Rout the bottom mortises on the front rail. Then put the spacer between the rail and vertical clamping surface on the jig. This moves the rail out so you can rout the top mortises. I rout the entire through-mortise from one side of the rail, taking shallow cuts (about ⅛ in.). I don't use a backer block because I've never experienced tearout with this type of end mill (it is an up-cutting bit). Just don't take too big of a cut.

Now rout the mortises in the side rail's end grain, adjust the jig's stop block, and rout the double mortises that join the back rail to the side rails. Then set up to rout the vertical mortises in the front legs. Put a ⅜-in.-dia., two-flute aluminum cutting end mill in the router and adjust the jig to center the mortises on 1¼-in.-thick material. Once that's done, adjust the jig to center the bit on ⅞-in.-thick material and rout the matching mortises in the end grain of the front rail.

Finally, rout the mortise in the back leg for the integral tenon on the side rail. The tenon is stepped, with a large base section that carries the weight and a pair of smaller wedged through-tenons that lock the joint. Rout the mortise for the tenon's base first and then the two through-mortises.

Two-part cheeks. After cutting thinner cheeks at the end of the board, lower the dado set, adjust the rip fence, and cut the thicker base section of the tenon.

Form the double tenon. The author makes all of the cuts at the bandsaw, using diagonal cuts to clean out the waste between the tenons.

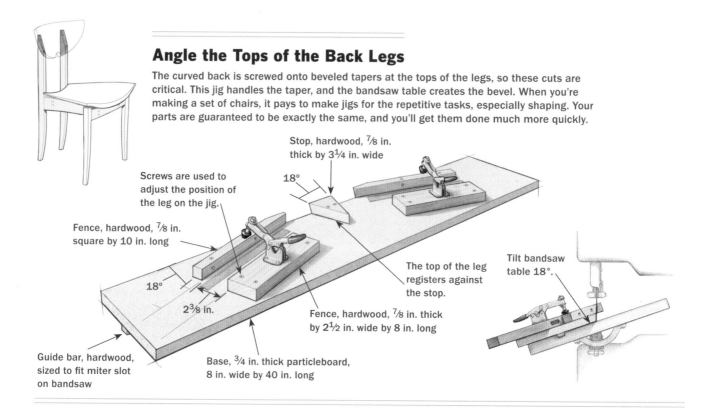

Angle the Tops of the Back Legs

The curved back is screwed onto beveled tapers at the tops of the legs, so these cuts are critical. This jig handles the taper, and the bandsaw table creates the bevel. When you're making a set of chairs, it pays to make jigs for the repetitive tasks, especially shaping. Your parts are guaranteed to be exactly the same, and you'll get them done much more quickly.

Stop, hardwood, ⅞ in. thick by 3¼ in. wide

18°

Screws are used to adjust the position of the leg on the jig.

Fence, hardwood, ⅞ in. square by 10 in. long

18°

2⅜ in.

The top of the leg registers against the stop.

Fence, hardwood, ⅞ in. thick by 2½ in. wide by 8 in. long

Tilt bandsaw table 18°.

Guide bar, hardwood, sized to fit miter slot on bandsaw

Base, ¾ in. thick particleboard, 8 in. wide by 40 in. long

Time for tenons

To make the slip tenons, start with two blanks milled to the final thickness and width. Rip a groove down both faces of one blank. The grooves give the glue a place to go. Next, round over the edges of both blanks to match the ends of the mortises. Finally, cut individual slip tenons from the blanks. For the tenons that fit a stopped mortise on one end only, use a handsaw to cut a small kerf (with the grain) on that end. Now cut the integral tenon into the side rail. Start at the tablesaw, cutting the cheeks with a dado set. Then head to the bandsaw and cut the two small through-tenons. Finally, cut slots in the tenons for the wedges and make the wedges.

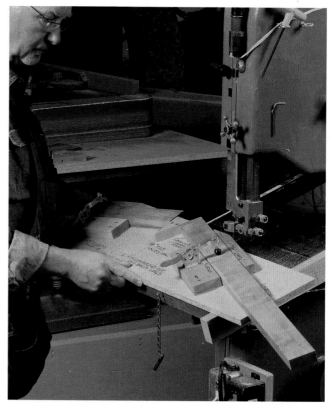

One jig, two legs, two angles. The angled table (18°) and jig combine to cut a compound angle on both legs in one shot. A wooden guide bar on the bottom rides in the table's miter slot.

Curve the Front Legs

The author bandsaws all the curves on these chairs, cleaning up with hand tools where possible. For concave surfaces, he uses router templates.

Roundovers on the router table too. The author uses part of a ¾-in. radius roundover bit to put a softer edge on these front legs. The pin at rear helps him enter the cut safely.

Clean up with a router. A flush-trimming bit leaves a clean, fair surface.

Shape the parts and assemble the base

Now shape the legs and rails. Start with the side rails, which have a beveled taper on their top edges to accommodate the curved seat. (The beveled edge sits higher than the front legs and rail so the seat clears them.) Then cut the compound taper at the top of the back legs to fit the curved back. Clean it up with a block plane.

Next, cut the curves on the legs. Trace the profile from a full-size template, rough out the shape at the bandsaw, and then clean up the curves. Convex curves are easily smoothed with a handplane, but concave curves are trickier. For those, I use a template and rout the parts flush to it at the router table, making sure always to rout down the curve and with the grain.

Now Taper the Legs

With their curves cut, the author bevels and tapers the legs with sleds. He holds them in place by hand, reaching past the blade when necessary.

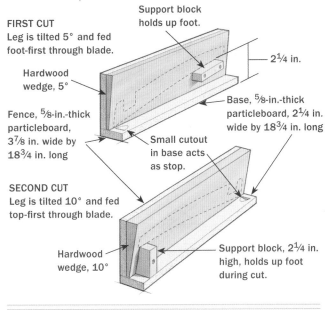

FIRST CUT
Leg is tilted 5° and fed foot-first through blade.

Support block holds up foot.

Hardwood wedge, 5°

2¼ in.

Fence, ⅝-in.-thick particleboard, 3⅞ in. wide by 18¾ in. long

Base, ⅝-in.-thick particleboard, 2¼ in. wide by 18¾ in. long

Small cutout in base acts as stop.

SECOND CUT
Leg is tilted 10° and fed top-first through blade.

Hardwood wedge, 10°

Support block, 2¼ in. high, holds up foot during cut.

The front legs are also tapered along their length and across their width. Both tapers can be done at once at the bandsaw. I use an L-shaped jig that has a tapered shim added to its vertical side.

The rails are much easier to shape. Just trace the curve onto the bottom edge, cut it out at the bandsaw, and rout it flush to a template at the router table.

After shaping the legs and rails, assemble the base. Glue the front rail to the front legs. Next, glue the side rails to the back legs. Wedge the tenons. Then glue the back rail between the two side rails and wedge those tenons. This creates an assembly made up of the back legs, back rail, and side rails. Let the glue dry. Finally, glue and wedge the side rails into the front rail. After the glue has dried, trim all of the wedges and tenons, cutting them close with a handsaw and handplaning them flush.

Wedge-shaped fence is the key. Tilting the leg into the blade creates an angle on the side, and raising the foot (pushing it farther out than the leg's top) cuts a taper along the leg's length.

Second jig for the second side. The wedge's angle is double that on the first jig, and the leg is fed through the blade top-first, so it's raised on the trailing end.

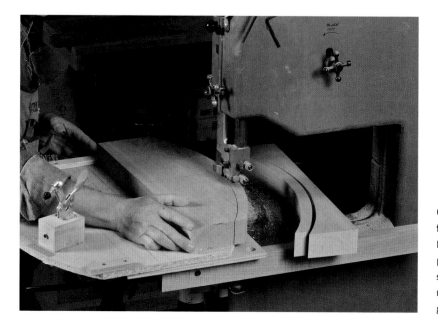

Cut the back's inside curve first. No clamps are needed because the force of the cut pushes the blank against the stop. But as the blank gets narrower, use a bit of hot-melt glue on the leading end.

Curved Seat and Back: Stack and Conquer

Rather than cooper the curved seat and back or sculpt them from solid slabs, both tedious techniques, the author cuts curved sections on the bandsaw and then simply stacks them. Little cleanup is required.

ANOTHER INGENIOUS JIG
You'll need two of these, one to form the curved sections for the seat and the other to handle the slightly different curve of the back. Both jigs work the same. The seat jig is 24 in. wide by 36 in. deep with reference lines 1⅛ in. apart. The one for the back is 21 in. wide by 19 in. deep, with reference lines 1 in. apart.
*See the plan on p. 128 for the radii.

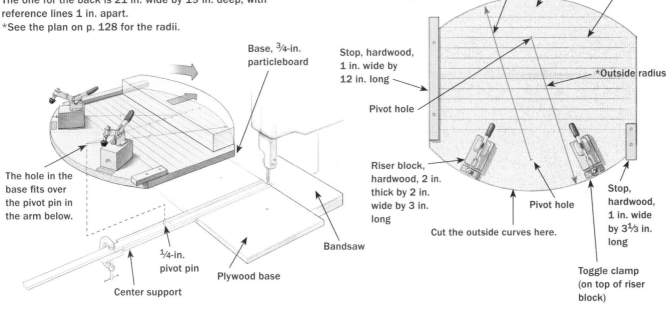

Base, ¾-in. particleboard

Stop, hardwood, 1 in. wide by 12 in. long

Pivot hole

Riser block, hardwood, 2 in. thick by 2 in. wide by 3 in. long

The hole in the base fits over the pivot pin in the arm below.

¼-in. pivot pin

Center support

Plywood base

Bandsaw

Cut the inside curves here.

*Inside radius

*Thickness lines

*Outside radius

Cut the outside curves here.

Pivot hole

Stop, hardwood, 1 in. wide by 3⅓ in. long

Toggle clamp (on top of riser block)

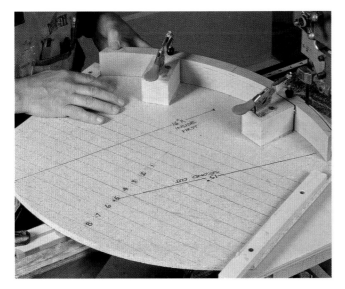

Other side now. The other side of the jig has a smaller radius, so the blank ends up thinner at the edges than in the center, eliminating the need to taper it by hand.

The secret to a comfortable seat

A chair is either made or broken by how comfortable it is. With traditional methods, shaping the seat and back for comfort is difficult, but the technique I use on this chair makes it easy.

Both the back and seat are made by cutting curved ribs from large blanks and then stacking them on edge and gluing them together to create a curved blank. The concave side becomes the scoop that your back and backside rest against.

Because both the back and seat are made in the same way, I'll show you how to make only the back. Start with a flatsawn board. The grain exposed by the bandsaw cuts will

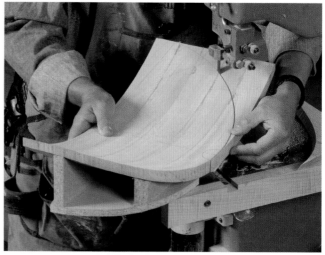

Cut it out at the bandsaw. Use hot-melt glue to hold the blank in place. The author puts the blank in the cradle first and then adds a few drops of glue along the seams.

Clamp it up in sections. The author starts by gluing up pairs of ribs and then glues those together into a single blank. Cauls across the blank's width keep the ribs aligned, which makes it much easier to smooth the blank.

complement the curve. Also, the board should be wide enough to make all of the ribs (use a second board for the seat).

To cut the curves, I use my bandsaw and a modified circle-cutting jig. It has a large base that pivots on a center point. The blank sits on top of the base as I feed it through the blade. I then advance the blank 1 in. closer to the blade and make a second cut to free another rib. Repeat until you've cut out all of the ribs. The outside curve is cut from the other end of the base, so rotate it, adjust the center point, and cut the curve on all of the ribs.

Next, edge-glue the ribs together to make the curved back blank. I do this in steps, first gluing up the ribs in pairs. Then glue all the

Use a Cradle for Controlled Cuts

Again, you need one cradle for the seat and one for the back.

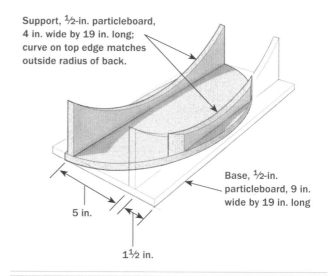

Support, ½-in. particleboard, 4 in. wide by 19 in. long; curve on top edge matches outside radius of back.

Base, ½-in. particleboard, 9 in. wide by 19 in. long

5 in.

1½ in.

Soften the edges. The author hogs off most of the waste with a Shinto saw rasp and then follows up with files (left) and sandpaper. To smooth the curves, use a sanding block that's been shaped to match the radius (right). Wrap the sandpaper around the ends of the block and staple it.

Slope the walls. Use a rat-tail file with a diameter that matches the bit used to rout the mortise—5/16 in. for all but the mortises on the back legs (use a 1/4-in.-dia. file there). An angled guide block ensures that the shape is correct.

Put glue in the mortises. Spread some on the area around the joint too, but not on the tenons. They'll swell and the joint will be much harder to fit. Assemble the front legs first. Elevate the parts and use shaped cauls to create a flat surface for clamping.

pairs together. After the glue is dry, I smooth the inside and outside curves using shopmade sanding blocks. I start with P120-grit sandpaper and work up to P220-grit.

Now shape the perimeter of the back. Because it's curved, you need a cradle to hold it: a piece of MDF for the base and two supports, both curved on the top edge to match the curve of the seat back. Draw the perimeter shape on the back and cut it at the bandsaw, with the table square to the blade. Sand the cuts smooth.

Finish the base, the seat, and the back. For a chair like this, I use Watco® Danish oil. Then screw the seat and back in place.

Then glue the side rails to the back legs.
Don't use a caul over the through-tenons. They need to stick out a bit for the joint to be pulled tight. Hammer in the wedges right away. After the glue is dry, the tenon won't spread for them. Also, sink them all the same amount so that after being trimmed flush to the leg they'll be the same thickness.

Easy to Change the Look

A café-style chair isn't right for every dining table, but by adding 1⅛ in. to the height of the back legs and adjusting the back's dimensions, you get a more traditional dining chair.

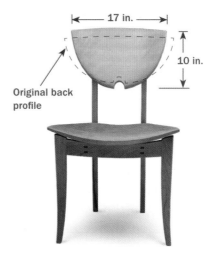

17 in.

10 in.

Original back profile

Finish the base and attach the back. When gluing the back rail between the side rails, the author dry-fits the front leg assembly (1). Then, when gluing on the front legs, he clamps a board to the back rail so he can get a clamp on both sides of the two joints (2). Finally, the back gets pilot holes for the screws (3).

Build a Classic Corner Chair

W. MICKEY CALLAHAN

The corner chair, sometimes called a roundabout chair, became fashionable in England and America in the late 17th and early 18th centuries. Supposedly created for a gentleman to sit on while wearing his broad coat and sword, it may owe its name simply to the fact that it sits nicely in the corner of a room. Regardless, it provides today's sitter with an optimal amount of back and arm support, especially when writing at a table or a desk.

Though the chair has lots of curves, the construction is simple mortise-and-tenon joinery without the compound angles found on many chairs. If you aren't a confident carver, eliminate the shell and replace the ball-and-claw foot with a pad foot; you'll still have a very handsome chair.

Shapely legs for a shapely chair

The two side legs and the back leg transition into the arm supports, whereas the front leg terminates at the seat. Pay close attention to the end-grain orientation when you lay out the stock: The front leg should be oriented for a bull's-eye grain pattern on the exposed knee. The other legs should have straight, vertical grain.

Transfer your patterns onto 16/4 stock machined to 3 in. square, but leave enough length for two knee blocks per leg. The knee blocks serve primarily as a transition between the legs and the seat rails.

While the leg blanks are square, lay out and cut all the mortises, then create the tenons that enter the arm rail. All the tenon shoulders must be at the same elevation for the arm to fit flush. Cut around the perimeter of the blank using a dado blade. The tenon is not centered, so set the elevation of the blade carefully for each cut. Drill a 7/8-in.-dia. hole in a piece of scrap to use as a gauge when rounding the tenons.

Anatomy
of an Heirloom

This chair is loosely based on one that was made in New York around 1765. The cabriole legs, relief-shell carving, and curved front rails reflect the earlier Queen Anne period, whereas the ball-and-claw feet and intricate splats reflect the later Chippendale style.

Arm rail, $\frac{7}{8}$ in. thick

Tenon, $\frac{7}{8}$ in. dia. by $1\frac{3}{8}$ in. long

Crest rail, $1\frac{7}{8}$ in. thick by $2\frac{1}{16}$ in. wide

Back leg/back arm post, 3 in. sq. by $30\frac{1}{4}$-in. overall length

Shoe

SIDE LEG/ SIDE ARM

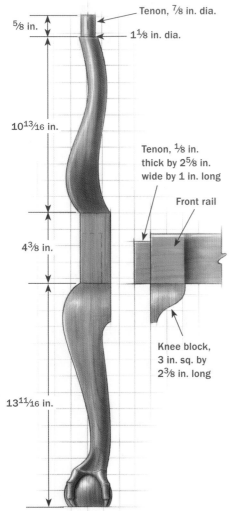

Tenon, $\frac{7}{8}$ in. dia.

$\frac{5}{8}$ in.

$1\frac{1}{8}$ in. dia.

$10\frac{13}{16}$ in.

Tenon, $\frac{1}{8}$ in. thick by $2\frac{5}{8}$ in. wide by 1 in. long

Front rail

$4\frac{3}{8}$ in.

Knee block, 3 in. sq. by $2\frac{3}{8}$ in. long

$13\frac{11}{16}$ in.

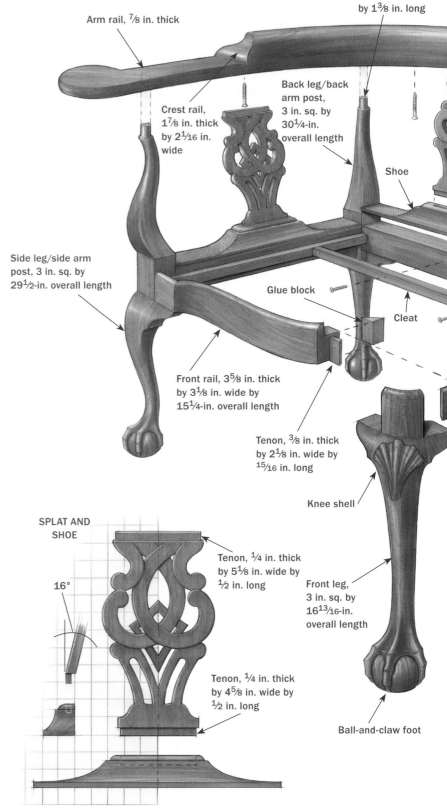

Side leg/side arm post, 3 in. sq. by $29\frac{1}{2}$-in. overall length

Glue block

Cleat

Front rail, $3\frac{5}{8}$ in. thick by $3\frac{1}{8}$ in. wide by $15\frac{1}{4}$-in. overall length

Tenon, $\frac{3}{8}$ in. thick by $2\frac{1}{8}$ in. wide by $\frac{15}{16}$ in. long

Knee shell

Front leg, 3 in. sq. by $16\frac{13}{16}$-in. overall length

Ball-and-claw foot

SPLAT AND SHOE

16°

Tenon, $\frac{1}{4}$ in. thick by $5\frac{1}{8}$ in. wide by $\frac{1}{2}$ in. long

Tenon, $\frac{1}{4}$ in. thick by $4\frac{5}{8}$ in. wide by $\frac{1}{2}$ in. long

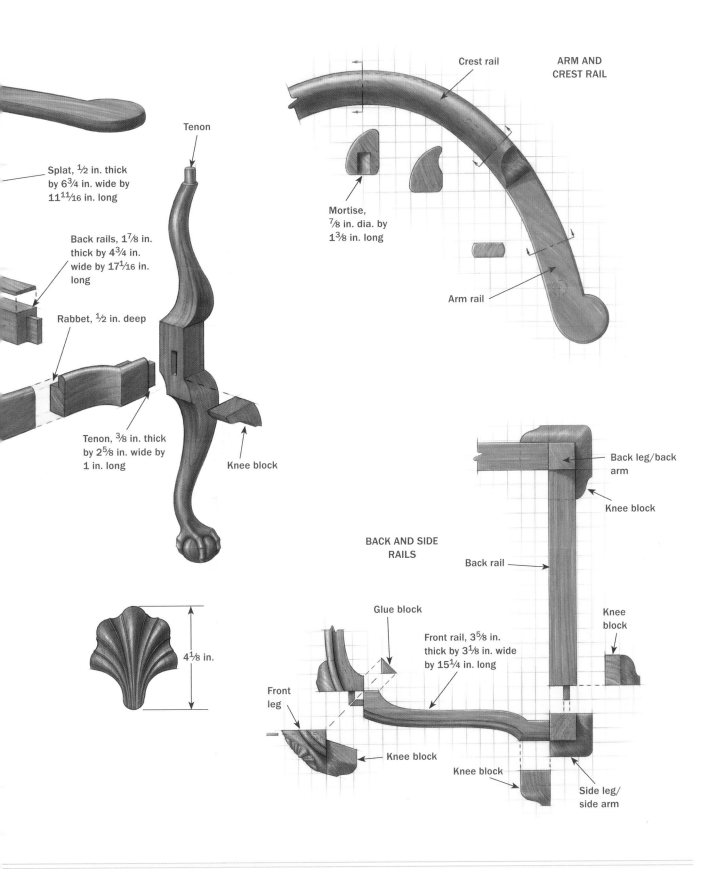

Splat, $\frac{1}{2}$ in. thick
by $6\frac{3}{4}$ in. wide by
$11\frac{11}{16}$ in. long

Tenon

Back rails, $1\frac{7}{8}$ in.
thick by $4\frac{3}{4}$ in.
wide by $17\frac{1}{16}$ in.
long

Rabbet, $\frac{1}{2}$ in. deep

Tenon, $\frac{3}{8}$ in. thick
by $2\frac{5}{8}$ in. wide by
1 in. long

Knee block

Crest rail

ARM AND
CREST RAIL

Mortise,
$\frac{7}{8}$ in. dia. by
$1\frac{3}{8}$ in. long

Arm rail

Back leg/back
arm

Knee block

BACK AND SIDE
RAILS

Back rail

Knee
block

$4\frac{1}{8}$ in.

Glue block

Front rail, $3\frac{5}{8}$ in.
thick by $3\frac{1}{8}$ in. wide
by $15\frac{1}{4}$ in. long

Front
leg

Knee block

Knee block

Side leg/
side arm

Legs first. Chair construction begins with the legs. Lay out the pattern, cut the joinery, and then shape the legs at the bandsaw with hand tools. Use a dado set to cut the leg tenons. While the leg blanks are still square, cut the tenons on the tops of the side and back legs that connect them to the arm rails.

Round the tenons. Guided by a drilled template, round the square tenons using chisels and carving gouges.

Cabrioles, back to back. The back and side legs are really two cabriole legs in one. Careful bandsawing now (top) will reduce hand shaping later (above). Chisels, rasps, files, and spokeshaves can all bring the legs to their final shape.

Cut away the knee-block stock and then rough out the cabriole legs on the bandsaw. Cut the square sections housing the mortises proud of the pattern because you will flush them to the fronts of the glued-in seat rails later. This is particularly important for the front leg because you will remove a large amount of stock, and leaving it square also aids clamping the leg to the rails.

Shape the legs and carve ball-and-claw feet, but hold off on the knee shell until the post of the front leg is rounded into the adjoining seat rails.

Curved rails, square joinery

Try to get all the rails from one board for grain and color consistency. This is particularly important for the two front rails, which should be laid out end to end or book-matched for a pleasing pattern on the curved faces.

Starting with the front rails, lay out and cut the tenons, and then trace the front and back profiles on the top of each rail. Bandsaw close to the lines, then clean up the surfaces with a curved-sole spokeshave and cabinet scrapers. Leave extra material on the front at each end so you can fair the rail-to-leg joints after they are glued.

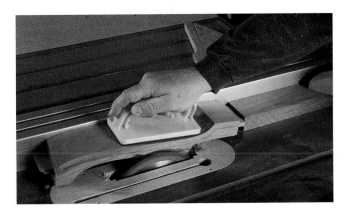

Front rails. The S-shaped front rails include a rabbet to support the upholstered seat. Start by rough-cutting the rabbet. Remove the bulk of the waste using a dado blade. Cut to the lowest point of the rabbet with one pass, clamp a stop block to the tablesaw and raise the blade into the stationary front rail, as shown, to make the deeper cuts.

The slip-seat frame is supported in the back by cleats, but it rests on a rabbet cut into the inside top faces of the front rails. To cut the rabbet, first lightly scribe a parallel line ½ in. from the front of each rail to establish its edge. Remove most of the waste with a dado blade, then trim to the scribe line using a gouge and chisel. Again, leave a little extra to be removed adjacent to the front leg after glue-up.

The two rear rails also incorporate a shoe that will house the bottom of the back splat. The shoe starts out as part of the back rail but is cut away. This ensures a perfect

grain match and provides a bigger section to handle when shaping the shoe.

Before cutting the tenons, use a router table to shape the cove and the quarter-round bead on the front face and top edge of each shoe. Now cut the tenons on each end and cut the shoes' side profiles on the bandsaw. Finish shaping them with a chisel and scraper. Excavate the mortise in the top of each shoe and then carefully carve the bead returns at each end of the mortise. When both shoes are profiled, saw them from the rear rails.

Dry-fit the four legs to the seat rails to ensure that all joinery is correct and that all four legs land firmly on the floor.

One long arm made from three parts

The construction of the arm rail is simplicity itself: The bottom two parts are butt-joined and held together by the crest rail. The arc of the arm is not a constant radius, so use care when laying out the parts.

To ensure matching profiles, nest the two arm blanks together using double-faced tape and rough-cut them on the bandsaw. Clean them up on the router table using a template and a bearing-guided bit. Bandsaw the crest

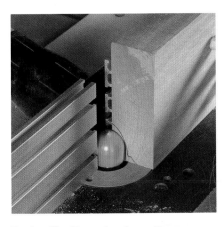

Back rails. Shape the shoes. Use a bullnose bit in a router table to cut the shoe's cove. Cut the bead with a corner-round bit.

Bandsaw the ends. With the front profile cut, draw the side profiles on the back of the shoe and cut them on the bandsaw.

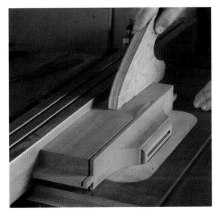

When you've finished shaping the shoes, cut them away from the back rails. Remove the small tab at each end.

Arm rail. The armrest flows around the back and sides of the chair. You need to locate the mortises accurately for the arm posts and the splats. To begin, shape the two sections of the arm, then screw them to the crest rail to act as a template for shaping it to match. Use a flush-trimming bit in the router table.

A tricky cut made easy. A hand screw provides a stable platform for bandsawing the ogee-shaped ends of the crest rail.

rail to rough shape. Using the arms as a template, clean up the crest rail on the router table, using a flush-trimming bit. Now cut the ogee-shaped ends on the bandsaw. Glue and screw the three parts together but leave any further shaping until later.

Once the glue dries, locate the mortises in the arm rail for the leg tenons. First, use the drawing to locate the mortise for the back-leg tenon and drill it on the drill press. Place the

tenon gauge you used earlier over the end of each side-leg tenon, and then use a Forstner bit to mark the center of each tenon. Use a clipped nail to drill a small hole in the center of each tenon. Inserting another clipped nail in each hole, place the dry-assembled chair base upside down on the arm rail. Align the two sections, push the nails into the rail, and drill mortises centered on the nail holes. You can now finish shaping the arm rail.

Trick for marking mortises. Use a clipped brad nail to drill a hole in the center of the side-leg tenons. Then place another clipped nail in the hole (above). Place the back leg tenon into its mortise in the arm rail. Set the side leg tenons an equal distance from the inside edge of the arm rail (right). Push down on the legs so that the nails mark the arm rail.

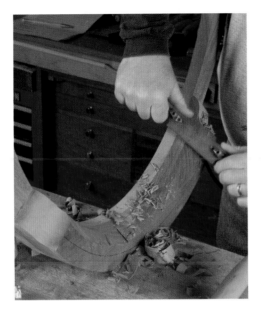

Finish shaping the crest rail. Use a flat chisel to rough out the front curve and then refine it using a spokeshave and scrapers (left). On the back side at both ends of the crest rail, use carving gouges to create the small, tapering recesses that are purely for ornamentation (above).

The back splats complete the chair

To make the back splats, first dry-fit the arm rail to the base to establish the distance between the top of the shoe and the arm rail. On a piece of scrap the same thickness as the back splats but an inch or two longer, cut an angled tenon that fits into the shoe. Rip off a ¼-in.-thick piece and crosscut it in two. Clamp these two parts so they overlap and use them as a measuring stick to determine the distance. Crosscut the scrap piece to this size and use it to mark the location of the mortises for the splats on the underside of the crest rail, including the center points.

Resaw the splats from one board, but leave them about 1 in. extralong. Because the mortises for both ends of the splats are perpendicular to the floor but the splats lean outward from the seat, you must angle the tenons accordingly.

With the same measuring stick used earlier, determine the total length of each splat, locate the tenon shoulders, and tweak the tenon angles. Transfer this information to the side of splats and cut them to final length with the ends at an angle of approximately 16°. Use an angled tenon jig to cut the tenons. Trim them to width with a handsaw and a bench chisel.

Once you are satisfied with the joints, spray-mount the pattern to the front of each splat. Bandsaw the outer profile and use a scrollsaw or fretsaw to cut the inner pattern. This design has an interlaced effect created by carving away material at the points of intersection. Make the initial cuts with the pattern attached, but remove it to complete the carving to get a better feel for the final look. Complete the splats by smoothing all the sawcuts and lightly chamfering all the exposed edges on the rear faces with curved and flat files.

Carve and shape as you assemble

Add the front knee blocks, which should fit flush to the bottom of the rail and the face of the adjacent leg post. Once fitted, simply rub-glue them into position. Sometimes a bed-spring clamp helps hold them in place until the glue sets up. Now glue the front rails to the front post, and then shape the front post to form a continuous curve. Then you can

How to get a perfect fit. Scraps help. Use a scrap of wood to find the height of the splat and the angle and location of the joinery.

Chop the mortise. Carefully clamp the arm rail so you can chop the splat mortises.

Angle the tenons with accuracy. Use a tenon jig and narrow dado set to form the tenons at each end of the back splats.

carve the knee shell and cut away the rabbet in the back of the front leg post for the seat frame.

I prefer to glue up the remainder of the base in two stages as it is less frantic and there is enough flex in the base to allow this. Because you can't use the front leg post for clamping when gluing on the side legs, you'll need to attach clamping blocks to the front rails. These are simply sandpaper-backed blocks attached with a separate clamp. Once this assembly is dry, add the back leg and the back rails.

Now assemble the top half of the chair. Dry-fit all the parts. If necessary, plane off some of the base of the shoes to get the shoes and splats to fit. Glue the shoes to the back rails, glue the splats into the shoes, and then glue the arm rail to the leg tenons and the top of the splats. You may require several bar clamps to ensure that the arm rail is firmly attached and flush to the shoulders of the two side and rear legs as well as the top shoulder of each splat.

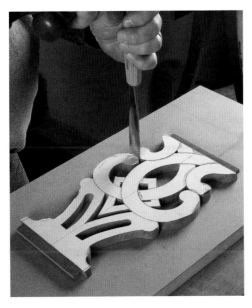

Carving tips. To give a three-dimensional look to the back splat, carve away material where the pattern intersects. After making the initial chop cuts at each intersection (above), remove the paper pattern and complete the carving (right).

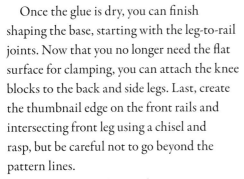

Once the glue is dry, you can finish shaping the base, starting with the leg-to-rail joints. Now that you no longer need the flat surface for clamping, you can attach the knee blocks to the back and side legs. Last, create the thumbnail edge on the front rails and intersecting front leg using a chisel and rasp, but be careful not to go beyond the pattern lines.

Glue and screw the seat-frame supports inside the back rails and add a small angled glue block inside the front leg and front rail intersection for added strength.

Make the slip-seat frame for upholstering the chair. Give the chair a final hand-sanding and then apply your choice of finish. I brushed on several washcoats of garnet shellac and then several coats of an oil/varnish mixture.

Assembly: Clamp, Then Shape

Keep the front leg post square to provide a flat surface for clamping the front rails to it. After glue-up, you can also extend the seat-frame rabbet onto the back of the front post.

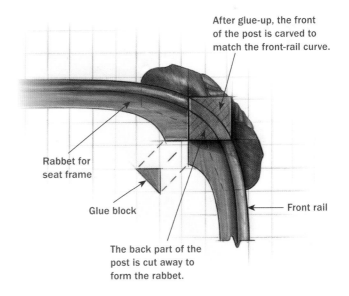

After glue-up, the front of the post is carved to match the front-rail curve.

Rabbet for seat frame

Glue block

Front rail

The back part of the post is cut away to form the rabbet.

Finish shaping the front post. After you have clamped on the front rails, you can extend their curve and rabbet onto the post.

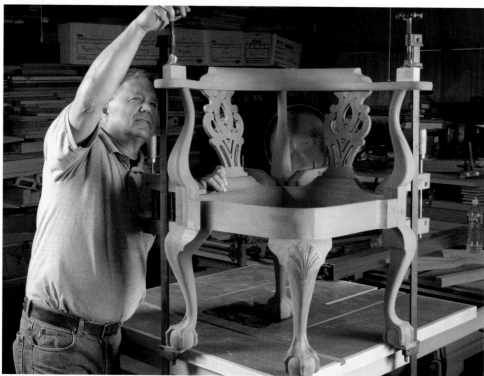

Final assembly. Clamping the arm/crest rail to the rest of the chair can be tricky given the chair's numerous curves. Do a dry-fit first. The easiest way to fine-tune the fit is to plane a bit off the shoes at the base of each back splat.

Arts and Crafts Side Chair

KEVIN RODEL

I designed this chair in 1993 for a design competition sponsored by the Maine Arts Commission. My intention was to design a chair that would be sturdy, comfortable, and clearly derivative of Arts and Crafts styling but still compatible with contemporary interiors. Since then I have made many of these chairs with very little design change, including one set ordered by Disney Films in 1999 for the movie *Bicentennial Man.* This version is made of white oak, though I've made the same chair in cherry and walnut.

Because I wanted the chair to function either as a dining chair for long, leisurely meals or as a reading chair for a desk or

Curved Back Splat Is the Focal Point

This white oak Arts and Crafts style chair fits comfortably in a dining room or a library setting. Though primarily rectilinear, the chair has a curved back splat and some angled joinery, so there are some construction challenges. But jigs and templates help you handle the curves and angles.

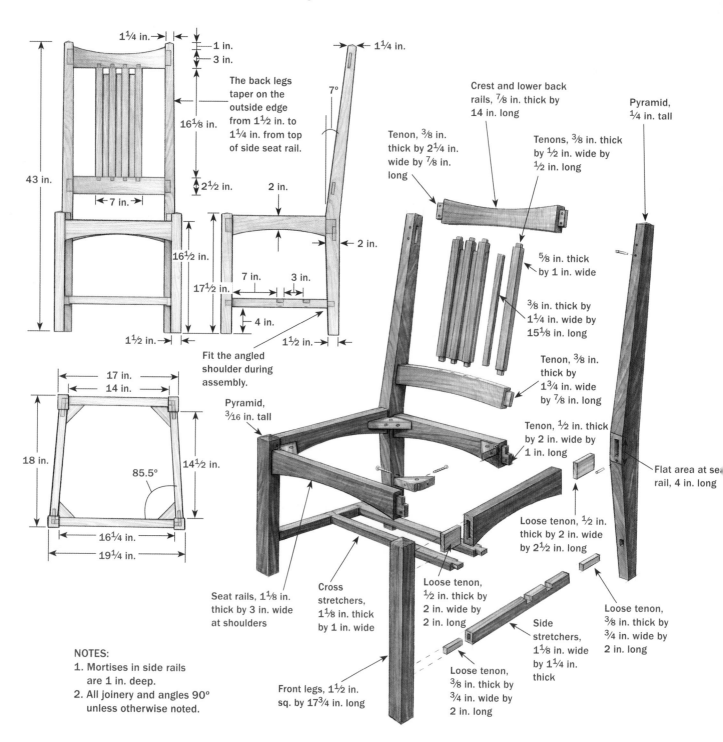

1¼ in.

1 in.

3 in.

1¼ in.

The back legs taper on the outside edge from 1½ in. to 1¼ in. from top of side seat rail.

7°

16⅛ in.

43 in.

2½ in.

7 in.

16½ in.

2 in.

2 in.

17½ in.

7 in.   3 in.

4 in.

1½ in.

1½ in.

Fit the angled shoulder during assembly.

Crest and lower back rails, ⅞ in. thick by 14 in. long

Pyramid, ¼ in. tall

Tenon, ⅜ in. thick by 2¼ in. wide by ⅞ in. long

Tenons, ⅜ in. thick by ½ in. wide by ½ in. long

⅝ in. thick by 1 in. wide

⅜ in. thick by 1¼ in. wide by 15⅛ in. long

Tenon, ⅜ in. thick by 1¾ in. wide by ⅞ in. long

17 in.

14 in.

18 in.

14½ in.

85.5°

16¼ in.

19¼ in.

Pyramid, 3/16 in. tall

Tenon, ½ in. thick by 2 in. wide by 1 in. long

Flat area at seat rail, 4 in. long

Loose tenon, ½ in. thick by 2 in. wide by 2½ in. long

Seat rails, 1⅛ in. thick by 3 in. wide at shoulders

Cross stretchers, 1⅛ in. thick by 1 in. wide

Loose tenon, ½ in. thick by 2 in. wide by 2 in. long

Side stretchers, 1⅛ in. wide by 1¼ in. thick

Loose tenon, ⅜ in. thick by ¾ in. wide by 2 in. long

Front legs, 1½ in. sq. by 17¾ in. long

Loose tenon, ⅜ in. thick by ¾ in. wide by 2 in. long

NOTES:
1. Mortises in side rails are 1 in. deep.
2. All joinery and angles 90° unless otherwise noted.

library table, an upholstered seat was a must. The degree of back slope, depth of seat area, arch or curvature of the back rest, and other critical dimensions also contribute to the comfort. I use jigs to duplicate curved and angled part as well as to create accurate angled joinery. These jigs will come in handy if you decide to build a set of chairs.

Shape the back legs using a template

First, trace the back legs on the stock using a full-size template made from ¼-in.-thick Masonite. Rough-cut the legs to shape using a jigsaw or bandsaw, being careful to leave the line. The only cuts that should be exactly to the line at this point are the top and bottom cross-grain cuts.

For final shaping, mount the back legs in a template-routing jig that works with both legs. Use a large-diameter, bearing-guided

straight bit (½ in. or more). Amana® makes a 1⅛-in.-dia. by 1½-in.-long bit with a top-mounted ball-bearing guide (part No. 45468) that allows you to shape the leg in one pass.

Once you have both rear legs shaped, cut the front legs to length. Now you're ready to lay out and cut the mortises.

Angled mortises made easy

It is certainly easier to cut right-angled, 90° mortises and tenons. But to conform to the body, the chair must have some angled joinery. I've limited the angled joints to the side rails and the lower side stretchers.

The easiest and most consistent way to cut the angled joint is to bore the mortise in the leg at the required angle. Then you can simply crosscut the ends of the adjoining rails at the same angle, cut a straight mortise into the end grain of the rails, and glue in a slip tenon.

Clamp the jig to a bench to rout the leg shape. A long bearing-guided bit can do the job in one pass; a shorter bit requires you to flip the jig and make two passes.

Two-Sided Jig for Routing Back Legs

Each leg is secured in the jig by screwing into the areas to be mortised, so mark out mortise locations on both faces.

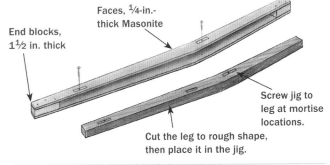

Faces, ¼-in.-thick Masonite

End blocks, 1½ in. thick

Screw jig to leg at mortise locations.

Cut the leg to rough shape, then place it in the jig.

Router Box Simplifies Mortising

This jig allows you to cut angled and straight mortises in the legs with a plunge router. It also allows for mortising for the loose tenons in the ends of the side rails.

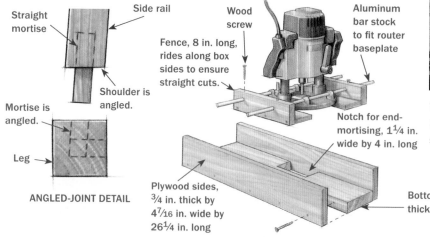

Straight mortise

Side rail

Shoulder is angled.

Mortise is angled.

Leg

ANGLED-JOINT DETAIL

Wood screw

Fence, 8 in. long, rides along box sides to ensure straight cuts.

Aluminum bar stock to fit router baseplate

Notch for end-mortising, 1¼ in. wide by 4 in. long

Plywood sides, ¾ in. thick by 4⁷⁄₁₆ in. wide by 26¼ in. long

Bottom, 1¼ in. thick by 3½ in. wide

Wedge leg in box for mortising. Adhesive-backed sandpaper prevents the wedges from slipping.

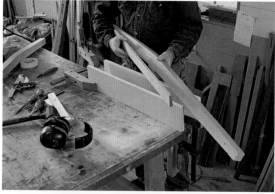

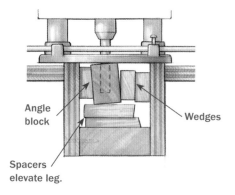

Use an Angle Block for Side-Rail Mortises

Angle block

Wedges

Spacers elevate leg.

Angle block orients the leg at 85.5°. Set the block against one side of the leg before adding the wedges. Then cut the mortise with a plunge router.

The angled mortises in the front and rear legs can be cut using a plunge router and a router mortising box. You can use the mortising box, a mortiser, or chisels to cut the straight mortises.

Now add the decorative details on the rear legs. Taper the outside faces on the bandsaw and plane to the line. Cut the shallow pyramid heads on both the front and rear legs. Finally, cut the mortises for the square pegs in the crest rail.

Use the Box for End Grain Too

The front and back rails meet the legs at 90° and have standard tenons. But the side rails meet the legs at an angle. Instead of cutting angled tenons, mortise for slip tenons.

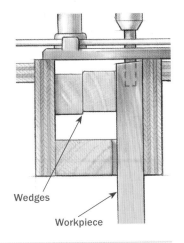

Wedges

Workpiece

Start by angling the ends of the rails. Cut the side rails to length at 85.5°, paying careful attention to the orientation of the angle cuts.

Side rails meet the legs at an angle

With the legs complete, begin working on the seat rails—front, back, and side. The rail-and-seat structure takes the brunt of the load, so use care when fitting the tenons.

The front and back rails meet the legs at 90° and have standard tenons. The side rails, which are angled into the front and back legs, are attached with slip tenons.

Cut the side rails to length at 85.5° at the shoulder line. The rail should look like a long, thin parallelogram, not a trapezoid. Next, lay out and cut the mortises on the ends for the slip tenons using the router box. After mortising, fit and glue the loose tenons into the side rails.

Template ensures consistent curves in all the rails

You want the arches in the chair rails to be consistent, so cut them to shape using templates made of ¼-in. Masonite. You'll need three templates for the seat-rail arches: one each for the front, sides, and back. Use the templates to draw the arch on the seat rails, then use a bandsaw to remove most of the waste. Now use a bearing-guided straight bit to template-rout the arches.

Mortise the ends of the rails. These mortises are easily cut by wedging the rail vertically in the router box.

Square up the mortises. Use a chisel and mallet and pare to the line.

Glue the loose tenons in the side rails. The tenon should fit with a bit of hand pressure. If you have to beat on it with a mallet, the fit is too tight; if it drops out, it is too loose.

Now rout the side-rail arches. Rough-cut the curve on the bandsaw. For consistency, screw a router template to the tenons, and secure the assembly to the bench for routing.

The two curved back rails require a few more steps than the seat rails. Mill up extrathick blanks and cut the offset tenons on the ends. For consistency, it helps to make a template showing both the inside and outside curves of the rail. Trace the concave curve first, then remove the waste with a bandsaw and clean up the surface using a spokeshave or sandpaper. If you prefer, you can use the template to make a jig to clean up the surfaces using either a router or shaper. Now use a marking gauge to scribe the 7/8-in. thickness of these rails, referencing off the just-milled front faces.

Before shaping the crest and bottom rails further, lay out and cut the four small mortises for the back splat.

The next operation is to arch the top of the crest rail using the same method and template used to shape the back seat rail (save the cutoff). Finally, cut the convex curves of the crest and bottom rails on the bandsaw, just leaving the line. Clean up these faces with a disk or belt sander.

Make the Back-Rest Assembly

The rails of the back rest are curved on the front and back faces, and the crest rail is arched on its top edge. Both rails are mortised to hold the back splat, a curved assembly of narrow strips.

CREST RAIL AND LOWER BACK RAIL LAYOUT

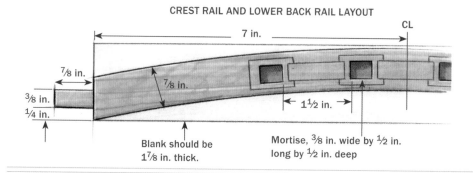

7 in.

CL

7/8 in.

7/8 in.

3/8 in.

1/4 in.

1 1/2 in.

Blank should be 1 7/8 in. thick.

Mortise, 3/8 in. wide by 1/2 in. long by 1/2 in. deep

Cut the tenons and the inside curve of the rails before mortising. Mark the locations of the back-splat mortises using a template and drill them out on the drill press (left). A curved fence helps support the tall workpiece. Next, following the lines marked from the template, square up the mortises (right).

Arch the top of the crest rail next. Reuse the rear seat rail template to trace the arch along the top of the crest rail, then rough out the shape on the bandsaw.

Back splat serves as the focal point

The back splat is a curved assembly of 1-in.-wide strips, with three 1-in.-sq. openings at the top, that conforms to the shape of the crest rail and the back rail. For this element, you'll need two blanks, ⅜ in. and ⅝ in., thick and wide enough to cut the required number of strips.

Dry-fit the crest rail and the back rail into the legs and measure vertically between them. Add 1 in. to that measurement for the ½-in. tenons, and cut the ⅝-in.-thick blank to length. Now cut ⅜-in.-thick tenons on each end, rip the board into four 1-in.-wide strips and then cut the remaining tenon shoulders on the strips. Next, cut the grooves for the ⅜-in.-thick strips, beginning 1 in. from the top shoulder line, and square up the top edge with a chisel.

Now cut the ⅜-in.-thick blank to the same length as the grooves, rip it into strips, and joint a 2° bevel along each edge of the thin strips. Sand all the parts to P220-grit and glue up the back splat using the crest rail and bottom rail as glue-up jigs. To avoid squeeze-out, use a glue syringe to apply the glue.

Finally, cut the curves on the backs of the top rails. Leave the scribe line, and clean up the surfaces with a belt or disk sander.

Glue up the front and rear assemblies

While the back-rest assembly is drying, glue up the two front legs and the front seat rail. Notch the tenon on the front rail to give clearance for the side-rail tenons. Be sure the legs are parallel with no toe-in or splay as you clamp up the assembly. Reinforce the joints with a ³⁄₁₆-in.-dia. dowel hidden on the inside face.

Mill and Glue Up the Back Splat

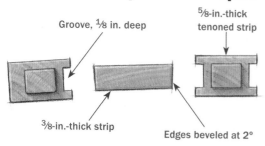

Groove, ⅛ in. deep

⅝-in.-thick tenoned strip

⅜-in.-thick strip

Edges beveled at 2°

Cut and fit the ⅝-in.-thick strips into the mortises in the rails, then rout the ⅜-in.-wide groove, ⅛ in. deep, into their edges. The outside strips are grooved only on the inside edge.

Bevel the thin strips. After ripping the ⅜-in.-thick strips to width, joint a 2° bevel on their edges to allow the splat to curve.

When the glued-up back splat has cured, remove the crest and back rails, apply glue to the mortises, and glue these parts together. To help with the clamp-up, use the arch cutoff as a caul.

Allow this assembly to dry, then glue it and the back seat rail to the rear legs. Again, reinforce the rear seat tenons on the inside with a ³⁄₁₆-in.-dia. dowel. While you are at it, install the ³⁄₁₆-in. pegs in the tops of the rear legs through the ¼-in.-sq. peg holes to reinforce the crest rail mortise-and-tenon joint.

Use the rails to guide the glue-up. Apply glue with a syringe to avoid squeeze-out. Do not glue the splat to the rails yet. Once the back splat has dried, glue it to the crest and bottom rails, then assemble the rest of the back.

Install the lower stretcher assembly

Not only does the lower stretcher assembly help stabilize the lower part of the chair against racking forces but the exposed dovetail joints also add a decorative twist. The side stretchers connect to the legs with slip tenons, and the cross stretchers are attached to the side stretchers with half-lapped dovetails.

With the chair dry-fitted and clamped together on a flat surface, measure and cut the lower stretchers to width and thickness. The side stretchers meet the legs at compound angles with slip-tenon joinery. The mortises are already cut. To cut the compound angle on the ends of the stretchers, set a bevel square to the angle formed where the inside face of the rear leg and the flat surface meet. Set the tablesaw's miter gauge to that angle, set the blade to 85.5° (double-check that angle with another bevel gauge) and cut the compound angle on the rear end of one stretcher. To cut the opposite stretcher, reset the miter gauge past

The rear shoulders of the stretchers are angled 85.5° horizontally. They must also be angled vertically to match the leg taper. Dry-clamp the chair, and set a bevel gauge to the vertical angle.

To cut the rear shoulder on the tablesaw, tilt the blade to 85.5°, then use the bevel gauge to set the angle of the miter gauge.

90° to the same angle in the other direction. Now cut the forward ends of the stretchers at 90°—with the miter gauge at 90° and the blade still at 85.5°—sneaking up on the length until they just fit.

Next, cut a ³⁄₈-in.-wide mortise, centered in the end grain of each stretcher and about ³⁄₄ in. deep. Dry-fit the slip tenons. When the fit is perfect, glue up the chair.

While this glue is setting, you can mill up the two cross stretchers. Once the stock is milled to width and thickness, locate where each cross stretcher will meet the side stretchers. Cut each one to length, leaving them about ¹⁄₈ in. extralong on both ends.

Hold a cross stretcher in place, and locate the shoulder cut by scribing a line on the underside where it meets the side stretcher.

Install the cross stretchers after glue-up. Cut the half-lapped dovetails on the cross stretchers, then scribe them onto the side stretchers.

Creep up on the fit. Reset the miter gauge to 90°, leaving the blade tilted to 85.5°, and cut the front shoulders. Leave each stretcher a little long and take light cuts until the ends align with the mortise locations.

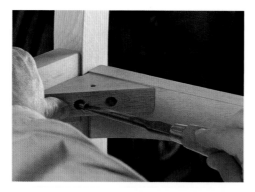

Screw in the corner blocks. The blocks help reinforce the corner joints and serve as anchors for the seat frame.

Cut a half-lapped dovetail on each end of each cross stretcher. Set the cross stretchers in place, then scribe and cut out the dovetail slots in the side stretchers using a handsaw and chisels. Once the dovetail sockets have been cleaned out, glue the cross stretchers in place.

After the glue has set, sand all the stretchers flush on their upper faces, and go over the chair thoroughly for any residual glue squeeze-out and touch-up sanding. Finally, make up the corner blocks and screw them to the inside corners, flush with the upper edges of the front and rear seat rails. Add an additional screw hole up through the body of the corner blocks before attaching them. This will be used to attach the upholstered slip seat to the chair.

The very last item before finishing is installing the pyramid-shaped decorative pegs in the crest rail. I use ebony, but any hardwood species will work.

This white-oak chair is fumed with a topcoat of Tried & True linseed oil. The seat is upholstered in leather purchased from Dualoy Leather (www.dualoy.com).

Last, the slip seat. The chair has a leather-upholstered seat, installed after the chair has been fumed and finished. The frame is screwed to the corner blocks between the rails.

Slip Seat Completes the Chair

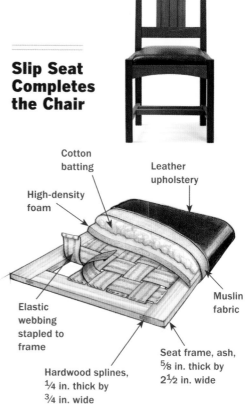

Cotton batting

Leather upholstery

High-density foam

Elastic webbing stapled to frame

Hardwood splines, ¼ in. thick by ¾ in. wide

Muslin fabric

Seat frame, ash, ⅝ in. thick by 2½ in. wide

A Bench That Fits Every Room

DANIEL CHAFFIN

I designed this bench to match a dining table, but its clean, contemporary style and comfortable seat let it sit just as well in the foyer, bedroom, mudroom, or on the front porch. It even works under a tree in the backyard, if made with exterior woods and finishes.

The slight taper on the tops of the seat slats complements their beveled edges. The legs, which are glued up from two boards, have a routed groove that both hides the glueline and ties the legs to the spaced seat slats. The legs also are arched along the bottom, a detail repeated on the stretchers.

These design details seem difficult, but they are surprisingly straightforward. Tapering the seat slats would be tough by hand, but I'll show you how a simple stick

Build It in a Weekend

Aside from the mortise-and-tenon joints, everything else—from tapers, grooves, and bevels to pocket screws—is simple to execute.

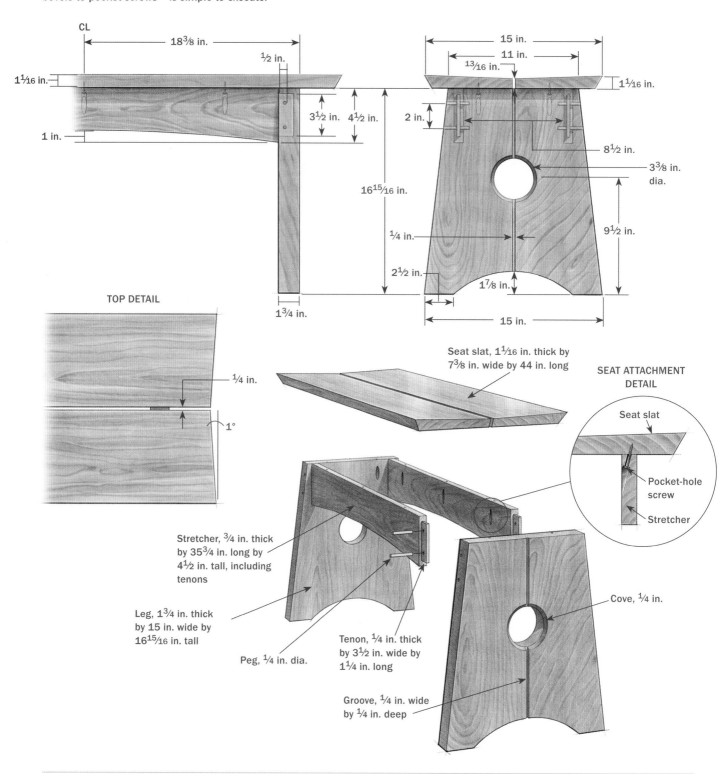

CL

18³⁄₈ in.

½ in.

1¹⁄₁₆ in.

3½ in.

4½ in.

1 in.

16¹⁵⁄₁₆ in.

1³⁄₄ in.

15 in.

11 in.

13⁄₁₆ in.

1¹⁄₁₆ in.

2 in.

8½ in.

3³⁄₈ in. dia.

9½ in.

¼ in.

2½ in.

1⁷⁄₈ in.

15 in.

TOP DETAIL

¼ in.

1°

Seat slat, 1¹⁄₁₆ in. thick by 7³⁄₈ in. wide by 44 in. long

SEAT ATTACHMENT DETAIL

Seat slat

Pocket-hole screw

Stretcher

Stretcher, ¾ in. thick by 35³⁄₄ in. long by 4½ in. tall, including tenons

Leg, 1³⁄₄ in. thick by 15 in. wide by 16¹⁵⁄₁₆ in. tall

Peg, ¼ in. dia.

Tenon, ¼ in. thick by 3½ in. wide by 1¼ in. long

Groove, ¼ in. wide by ¼ in. deep

Cove, ¼ in.

turns a planer into a tapering machine. Templates simplify the shaping of the legs and stretchers and make it easier to produce multiple benches.

Make a template for the legs

You could make the legs from a single 15-in.-wide board, but few people have a jointer and planer wide enough to handle it. I recommend using two narrower boards for each leg.

Leave some extra width on the boards. That will help keep the glueline centered so it will be hidden by the routed groove. Keep the boards a bit long as well, so there's room to adjust them for the best grain match. After gluing the boards together, joint one edge and rip the leg to width, keeping the glueline centered.

Making a template for the legs is time well spent. A Forstner bit large enough to cut the hole in the leg will leave tearout on the walls of the hole. The template allows you to drill the hole undersize and rout it to finished diameter with a spiral bit, leaving a smooth surface.

I guide the spiral bit with a bushing, so the hole in the template needs to be 3½ in. dia. to account for the offset and create a 3⅜-in.-dia. hole. The arc, on the other hand, is made with a bearing-guided, flush-trimming bit, so it should be actual size on the template. To draw the arc, use a ⅛-in.-thick batten made from quartersawn lumber. Register the ends of the batten against two small clamps, push it to its apex, and trace the arc.

Remove the waste at the bandsaw. Smooth the cut by sanding to the line. Bore the hole at the drill press and attach the fences.

Put that template to work

Use the template to mark the arc and hole on your leg stock. Then bandsaw and drill out the waste. Put the leg back in the template and secure it to the bench—I use holdfasts. There's no need for double-faced tape because the

Make the template. Attach three fences—one for the top and two for the sides—to align the legs in the template so they're marked and routed consistently. After attaching the first two, place the leg blank against them and use it to align the third.

A Template Makes Quick Work of the Legs

This template not only helps lay out the arc and hole before roughing them out but also works as a guide for your router, ensuring that both legs are the same and that the hole and arc are accurate and clean.

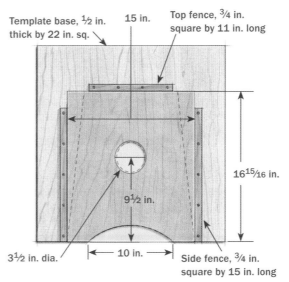

Template base, ½ in. thick by 22 in. sq.

15 in.

Top fence, ¾ in. square by 11 in. long

16¹⁵⁄₁₆ in.

9½ in.

3½ in. dia.

10 in.

Side fence, ¾ in. square by 15 in. long

three fences and clamping pressure hold the leg in place. Rout the arc and hole to final size.

I clean up the routed surfaces with a card scraper—using a narrow one for the hole—and sandpaper. While you have the router out, rout the cove detail on the show sides of the holes and then groove the center of the legs. Now mortise the legs. I do this before tapering them because I use a hollow-chisel mortiser to cut them and I want square edges to register against its fence. A router and edge guide would also work.

After all the mortises are cut, lay out the leg tapers with a straightedge and cut close to the lines at the bandsaw. Clean up the cuts with a smoothing plane. Mark the arc on the stretchers. I make a plywood template, using a batten to lay out the arc so they're the same. Cut the tenons and trim them to fit. Then cut the arc at the bandsaw and clean it up with a spokeshave.

Remove the waste before routing. Place the leg blank in the template, and trace the arc and circle onto its inside face (top left). Cut the waste from the arc, leaving about $\frac{1}{16}$ in. to be routed away (top right). For the hole, the author uses a $3\frac{1}{4}$-in. Forstner bit (bottom), which leaves about $\frac{1}{8}$ in. of waste. Any tearout on the outside is removed by the router.

Rout the arc. Because the legs are 1¾ in. thick, it takes two passes with a pattern bit to rout the arc flush. On the first pass, the bearing rides against the template. For the second pass, remove the template and register the bearing against the routed surface.

Simple stick tapers seat

Nearly every surface on the seat slats is beveled or tapered, and it's important to cut them in the right order. First, taper the slats' thickness. Then cut the compound angles on the ends. Finally, bevel the outside edges.

I've tapered the seat slats across their width with a handplane, but it took forever. I've also used an elaborate sled for my planer. Every taper I cut with it had to be fixed with a handplane, so I rethought my approach and came up with a simple solution—so simple, I wonder how I could have missed it earlier.

All you need so that your planer will make this cut time after time is a stick that lifts the inside edge of the slat higher than the outside edge. Ironically, the stick I use is an offcut from the elaborate sled. Attach the stick to the bottom of the slat on the inside edge with double-faced tape and use a pencil to mark

Rout the Arc

FIRST PASS

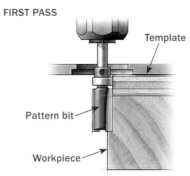

Template

Pattern bit

Workpiece

SECOND PASS

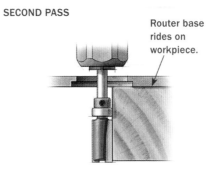

Router base rides on workpiece.

Rout the Hole with a Single Pass

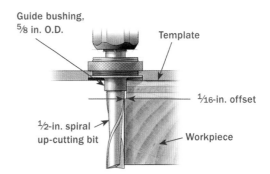

Guide bushing, ⅝ in. O.D.

Template

½-in. spiral up-cutting bit

1⁄16-in. offset

Workpiece

Rout the hole. A 2-in.-long spiral bit cuts end grain and long grain cleanly and is long enough to trim the walls in one pass.

Cove the edge. A ¼-in. bearing-guided cove bit routs a nice detail on the outside edge of the hole.

lines over its entire face. When the last bit of pencil has been removed, you're done. It's that simple.

With the ends still square, clamp the slat between benchdogs and plane all the surfaces smooth.

Tilt the tablesaw blade to 60°, adjust the miter-gauge fence to 89°, and crosscut the slats. Move the gauge to the other side of the table and flip the board onto its other face to cut the second end. With the blade still at 60°, bevel the outside of each slat.

Prep all the surfaces for finishing now. If you wait until after assembly, you'll find places that you can't get at well enough to do a good job, like between the stretchers. I use a smoothing plane and break the edges with a block plane. Because cherry is prone to blotching, I lightly sand all the parts with P320- or P400-grit sandpaper so that it absorbs the oil finish more evenly.

Groove the glueline. Use a ¼-in. straight bit to rout a ¼-in.-deep groove over the glueline.

Taper and bevel the seat. A flat seat isn't comfortable. Taper the slats across their widths so that they are thinner on the inside edge than the outside.

Taper First, Bevel Second

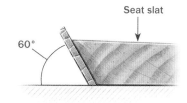

60°
Seat slat

Ends get a compound angle. With the blade tilted to 60° and the miter gauge set at 89°, crosscut the slat to length. The outside edge should be against the fence. For the second cut, move the miter gauge to the other side of the table and turn the board over.

A simple trick for big tapers. All you need to taper the seat slats is a ¼-in.-sq. stick. Attach it to the inside edge of the slat with double-faced tape. The author puts cross-hatching on the board to gauge his progress.

Edges last. Leave the blade at 60° and bevel the outside edge of the seat slat.

Assembly is straightforward. With only four joints, assembly isn't tough. Glue the base together, then peg the joints. To start, glue the stretchers to the legs. Spread glue on the tenons and tap them home. Scrape away the squeeze-out when the glue starts to gel, but leave the clamps on for a few hours.

Peg the joints. Saw off the waste and use a sharp block plane to bring them flush.

Add the seat. Secure the top with pocket-hole screws. Note the ¼-in.-thick spacer on the bench keeping the tapered slats flat against the legs.

Assemble and finish the bench

I use pocket screws—located on the inside of the stretchers and legs—to attach the seat slats. Cut the pocket holes before assembling the bench.

Begin the assembly by gluing and clamping the stretchers and legs together, making sure that their top edges stay aligned. Let the glue set for a few hours and then drill holes for the pegs that pin the tenons. I make cherry pegs with a dowel plate, but you also can buy them. Don't use much glue on the pegs. They're a tight fit in the holes, and the pressure created when you drive them in could force glue out through the faces of the legs. Cut the pegs close and plane them flush. Now place the slats on top of the legs, aligning their inside edges with the groove cut into the legs. Drive in the pocket screws and you're ready to finish the bench.

You can build this bench in a weekend, but the finishing might take longer. I applied three thin coats of Tried & True varnish oil,

Oil finish for warmth. Three coats of a linseed oil/varnish finish brings out the natural color of cherry and protects the seat.

wiping away excess oil after an hour. Allow plenty of time for each coat to dry before applying the next. In Kentucky, that can mean four days between coats in the summer, less in the winter. Buff the first coat with 0000 steel wool, and the last two with a soft cloth. Top it off with a coat of paste wax.

Contributors

Christian Becksvoort, a contributing editor to *Fine Woodworking*, builds furniture in New Gloucester, Maine. He has been doing restoration work at the Sabbathday Lake Shaker community since 1975.

W. Mickey Callahan is a custom period furniture maker in Bellingham, Mass. and the co-founder of the Society of American Period Furniture Makers.

Daniel Chaffin co-owns Daniel Chaffin Furniture Makers located in downtown Louisville, Ky., which focuses on original designs. The small company employs six people full-time and churns out a constant stream of new furniture and small products, all created with an eye for subtle details, inviting textures, and perfect finishes.

Kelly J. Dunton is a *Fine Woodworking* associate art director.

Charles Durfee builds furniture in Woolwich, Maine.

Dan Faia is a carver, cabinet maker, and chair maker. He is a graduate of the North Bennet Street School (NBSS) in Boston, Mass., and runs his own woodworking shop in New Hampshire. In addition, he is the department head of the full-time cabinet and furniture making program at NBSS. Visit him online at www.dcfwoodworking.com.

Michael C. Fortune, a *Fine Woodworking* contributing editor, has designed and built furniture for more than 30 years. He is one of Canada's most acclaimed contemporary furniture masters and was the first furniture maker to receive Canada's prestigious Bronfman Award for excellence in fine craft. He received the Award of Distinction from the Furniture Society in 2007. You can visit him online at www.michaelfortune.com.

Stephen Hammer designs and makes custom furniture in Wethersfield, Conn. You can visit him online at www.urbanforestfurniture.com.

Kevin Kauffunger is a furniture maker in Pittsburgh, Pa.

Gregory Paolini owns and operates a custom furniture and cabinetry business near Asheville, N.C. He also writes and teaches about woodworking. You can see examples of his work at www.GregoryPaolini.com.

Michael Pekovich is the art director for *Fine Woodworking* and a professional woodworker on weekends.

Kevin Rodel is a furniture designer with a studio in Brunswick, Maine. He also teaches part-time at several furniture schools around the country and is co-author of the book *Arts & Crafts Furniture: from Classic to Contemporary* (Taunton Press, 2005). You can visit him online at www.kevinrodel.com.

Mario Rodriguez is a longtime *Fine Woodworking* contributor who teaches at the Philadelphia Furniture Workshop (philadelphiafurnitureworkshop.com).

Gary Rogowski is the Director of The Northwest Woodworking Studio, a school for woodworkers, in Portland, Ore. He is a frequent contributor to several woodworking magazines and his latest book is called *The Complete Illustrated Guide to Joinery* (The Taunton Press, 2005).

Credits

All photos are courtesy of *Fine Woodworking* magazine © The Taunton Press, Inc., except as noted below:

Front cover: Main photo by Matt Kenney, left photos top to bottom: Michael Pekovich and Steve Scott.

Back cover from top to bottom: Michael Pekovich, Thomas McKenna, and Matt Kenney.

The articles in this book appeared in the following issues of *Fine Woodworking*:

pp. 4–11: Make a Limbert-Style Coffee Table by Gregory Paolini, issue 215. Photos by Matt Kenney except for photo p. 4 by Keith Wright. Drawings by John Hartman.

pp. 12–19: Coffee Table in Mahogany by Mario Rodriguez, issue 182. Photos by Tom Begnal. Drawings by Vince Babak.

pp. 20–31: Coffee Table Puts Joinery on Display by Kevin Rodel, issue 178. Photos by Matt Berger except for photos p. 20, p. 22, and p. 31 by Michael Pekovich. Drawings by John Hartman.

pp. 32–41: Shaker Classic Two Ways by Christian Becksvoort, issue 210. Photos by Anissa Kapsales except for photo p. 32 by Dennis Griggs. Drawings by David Richards.

pp. 42–51: Porringer-Top Tea Table by Dan Faia, issue 191. Photos by Steve Scott. Drawings by Bob La Pointe.

pp. 52–59: Arts and Crafts Side Table by Kelly J. Dunton, issue 186. Photos by Mark Schofield except for photo p. 52 by Michael Pekovich. Drawings by John Hartman.

pp. 60–69: Shaker-Inspired Hall Table by Christian Becksvoort, issue 227. Photos by Steve Scott except for photo p. 60 by Dennis Griggs. Drawings by Bob La Pointe.

pp. 70–81: A Graceful Hall Table by Kevin Kauffunger, issue 212. Photos by Mark Schofield. Drawings by Bob La Pointe.

pp. 82–91: Build a Bow-Front Hall Table by Charles Durfee, issue 204. Photos by Matt Kenney. Drawings by Bob La Pointe.

pp. 92–102: Build a Hayrake Table by Michael Pekovich, issue 226. Photos by Rachel Barclay except for photo p. 92 by Michael Pekovich; photos p. 93 and p. 95 by Mark Schofield; top left photo p. 102 by Gina Eide; and top right and bottom photos p. 102 by Steve Scott. Drawings by John Hartman.

pp. 103–109: Dining Table with Two-Way Drawers by Stephen Hammer, issue 219. Photos by Matt Kenney. Drawings by Stephen Hammer.

pp. 110–116: The Versatile Trestle Table by Gary Rogowski, issue 214. Photos by Michael Pekovich except for top left photo p. 116 by Steve Scott. Drawings by Dave Richards.

pp. 117–125: Shaker Dining Table by Christian Becksvoort, issue 193. Photos by Tom Begnal except for photos p. 117, p. 124, and p. 125 by Michael Pekovich. Drawings by Bob La Pointe.

pp. 126–138: A Revolution in Chairmaking by Michael C. Fortune, issue 227. Photos by Matt Kenney. Drawings by John Hartman.

pp. 139–148: Build a Classic Corner Chair by W. Mickey Callahan, issue 215. Photos by Mark Schofield. Drawings by Bob La Pointe.

pp. 149–158: Arts and Crafts Side Chair by Kevin Rodel, issue 190. Photos by Thomas McKenna except for bottom right photo p. 158 by Michael Pekovich. Drawings by Bob La Pointe.

pp. 159–166: A Bench That Fits Every Room by Daniel Chaffin, issue 207. Photos by Matt Kenney except for photo p. 159 by Matthew Frederick. Drawings by John Hartman.

Index